100 Ways to Beat the Credit Crunch

D1342393

This is a **FLAME TREE** book
First published in 2008

Publisher and Creative Director: Nick Wells
Project Editor: Cat Emslie
Art Director: Mike Spender
Layout Design: Jake and Mike Spender
Digital Design and Production: Chris Herbert
Picture Research: Cat Emslie, Toria Lyle
Proofreader: Siobhán O'Connor
Indexer: Penny Brown

Special thanks to Adrian Cole, Chelsea Edwards and Sara Robson

08 10 12 11 09
1 3 5 7 9 10 8 6 4 2

This edition first published 2008 by
FLAME TREE PUBLISHING
Crabtree Hall, Crabtree Lane
Fulham, London SW6 6TY
United Kingdom

www.flametreepublishing.com

Flame Tree is part of the Foundry Creative Media Co. Ltd
Text licensed to the Foundry and © the CashQuestions team
The authors assert their moral rights.

ISBN 978-1-84786-398-0

A CIP Record for this book is available from the British Library upon request

The authors have made all reasonable efforts to ensure that the information in this book is correct at the time of going
to print, and the publisher cannot accept any liability for incorrect or out-of-date information. The publisher would be glad to
rectify any omissions in future editions of this book.

All rights reserved. No part of this publication may be reproduced, stored in a retrieval system, or transmitted in any form or by any
means, electronic, mechanical, photocopying, recording or otherwise, without prior permission in writing of the publisher.

Printed in India

The picture on page 128 is © Foundry Arts/courtesy of Paul Forrester. All other pictures are courtesy of Shutterstock and © the following photographers: 5b & 62, 39, 148 Yuri Arcurs;
6t & 98, 111 Morgan Lane Photography; 10 Belinda Pretorius; 11, 138, 209, 216, 214 Monkey Business Images; 14 Alessio Ponti; 17, 24, 89 Karen Roach; 21 3dts; 23 Feng Yu; 27 Postnikova
Kristina; 29 Bartosz Ostrowski; 30 Michael Pettigrew; 31 Tia; 32 Hannamariah/Barbara Helgason; 34 Feverpitch; 36 David Hughes; 41 TAOLMOR; 43 Milos Jokic; 45 Valery Potapova;
47 Luminis; 49 Timothy R. Nichols; 51 Multiart; 52 Ewa B; 55 R. Mackay Photography; 59 Nigel Carse; 65 Copestello; 66 Michal Mrozek; 69 semenovp; 71 Infomages; 73 Tatjana Strelkova;
75 Amp; 77 Kirsty McNaught; 79 Sebastian Kaulitzki; 81 chlorophylle; 83 Nagy Melinda; 91 Norman Chan; 93 Grozaya; 95 300dpi; 96 cloki; 101 Graca Victoria; 102 Quayside; 103 mashe;
105 matka_Wariatka; 106 Jiri Miklo; 109 bravajulia; 112 Clay Kasserman; 115 Christopher Elwell; 116 Maksymilian Skolik; 119 Lukiyanova Natalia; 120 Robyn Mackenzie; 123 Fanfo;
127 rep0rter; 133 Tischenko Irina; 134 Gordon Swanson; 137 Petr Jilek; 140 Piotr Lukasik; 141 Marjan Veljanoski; 144 Jeffrey Van Daele; 146 Clement K.L. Cheah; 152 Galina Barskaya;
153 Knud Nielsen; 157 Chris Jenner; 159 BHE017; 163 Dmitrijs Mihejevs; 164 Stephen Strathdee; 167 Mike Brake; 170 Mikolay Okhitin; 173 Sergiy Zavgorodny; 175 Ken Brown; 176 L Kelly;
179 Radu Razvan; 183, 237, 245 iofoto; 184 Racheal Grazias; 187 Khafizov Ivan Harisovich; 189 Losevsky Pavel; 190 Lars Christensen; 193 Darren Baker; 195 Tom Davison; 198, 203 Rob
Wilson; 199 Andrjuss; 207, 235 Stephen Coburn; 213 Rafael Ramirez Lee; 218 Chris@; 219 spanovic; 221 Hau Haoang; 222 Oleinik Dmitri; 227 ragsac; 228 Lee Torrens; 232 Michelle D.
Milliman; 233 3445128471; 241 Countryroad; 242 Denis and Yulia Pogostins; 243 Chiyacat; 247 Sandra G; 248 George Allen Penton; 5t & 18 Yellowj; 6b & 124 Pinkcandy;
7b & 180 Keith A Frith; 7t & 150 Mikael Damiker; 8b & 238 RoJo Images; 8c & 224 Maxim S. Sokolov; 8t & 204 Kristian Sekulic

100

Foreword: Adrian Coles

Annie Shaw, Laura Howard
& Simon Read

CashQuestions.com
The UK's personal finance problem-solver

Ways to

Beat

the Credit

Crunch

**FLAME TREE
PUBLISHING**

Contents

Foreword ———————————————————— 10
Introduction ————————————————— 12

Personal Finance ———————————— 18

The first area of your life that you should take a good look at. Before making any great savings on shopping or utilities, for example, you must ensure that you have the best possible deals with your bank, mortgage provider, credit cards, insurance, loans and investments, to make sure what money you do have is working its hardest. This chapter also provides advice on budgeting and where to go to get more help.

62 ——————————————— Shopping

Shopping in general is the most obvious area where we see our money leaking away from us. Sometimes we shop on impulse, and this is clearly something that has to be resisted in these tough times. This chapter provides invaluable advice on some golden rules to follow. It offers guidance on shopping in the sales, where to go for discount shopping, store cards, online shopping, haggling, buying second-hand and even how to get hold of freebies!

Food — 98

Eating is essential to life, but we can all save money on food without resorting to bland, unsatisfying food. There is much that can be done, from packing your own lunch, avoiding takeaways and cutting out the lattes, to being wise in the supermarket by buying value brands when there is no difference in taste, buying unwrapped veg and avoiding the tempting displays and specialized 'children's food' that is in fact no different from adults'.

124 — Household & Utilities

Our home is our castle, and it should remain so through these difficult times. Cleaning does not have to be so expensive – all those bottles under the sink could probably be replaced with far fewer multipurpose bargain brands or even by home-made traditional tricks. Who knew white vinegar was so versatile?! Learn all about budget decorating and saving money with gardening, and don't forget about those heating bills – this chapter shows you how to get the best utilities deals.

150

Transport

The first important step that anyone can take in saving money on transport is to travel under their own steam – walking and cycling are not only free, but of course very good for you too. Free and discounted travel is available to everyone to a degree, on buses and trains throughout the country, and cheap flights can still be come by despite increased fuel costs. If you must use the car, there are many ways to cut costs – from choosing the right car and insurance, to saving money on petrol.

Holidays

180

A respite from the stresses and strains of everyday life is all the more essential while the credit crunch bites, and this chapter shows you how you can still take a break without breaking the bank. You don't even have to go away – create a holiday at home with activities and day trips. Or stay in the UK with cheap hotel deals or self-catering, or rediscover the joys of camping. If you need the guaranteed sun of overseas, then follow our advice on cutting costs for foreign travel.

Sport & Leisure

204

Exercise, fun and relaxation are as important as holidays for keeping our mind and body healthy. Learn here how to exercise and play sport for free or at a greatly reduced cost – even if you can't bear to drop the gym. Discover the route to great nights out (or in) on the cheap, and how to keep the kids amused.

224

Making Money from Home

If the day job isn't bringing enough in, and you've done all you can to maximize your saving, there are ways to earn a little extra cash. Whether it's selling all manner of clutter you may have, making your home itself work harder for you or taking advantage of your skills and spare time, you can always muster a few more pounds for your pocket.

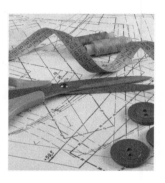

Gifts

238

We often forget to factor in the presents we have to buy for all manner of celebrations – so these are often the purchases which take us well over our budget. This chapter provides suggestions for making your own gifts – a gesture that is always appreciated for its personal value – as well as creating events and parties that will be far more memorable than material objects.

Websites & Further Reading 252

Index 254

Foreword

The term 'credit crunch' has now entered the nation's dictionaries. The closure of the wholesale money markets in August 2007 dislocated systems of making loans, gathering savings and financing house purchase around the world. It seems that banks don't trust each other any more – and they trust only their very best customers to repay their loans on time. In almost every developed country lending has fallen sharply since mid-2007, as so-called riskier borrowers are ignored. And, unbelievably, some banks have failed.

At the same time, food and fuel prices have rocketed. Rapid economic expansion in the developing world has increased the demand for oil and commodities. For many years cheap goods from abroad helped keep our inflation rates down; now the opposite is occurring and we are importing inflation from the rest of the world. At the same time economic growth here at home is falling, along with house prices, and unemployment is rising. The environment in which we work, play and shop has changed hugely in a very short period of time.

In the light of these powerful, impersonal, economic forces, how can the 'ordinary' consumer protect themselves and their families? A more careful choice of mortgage loans, credit cards, savings accounts and

insurance can save hundreds of pounds a year for many families. New shopping habits, different holidays, and a more sensible approach to driving are all ways of getting more for less.

However, it is difficult for any one family to come up with all the necessary ideas. This is where this comprehensive, up-to-date, guide comes in. Annie Shaw, Laura Howard and Simon Read from the highly respected CashQuestions.com have come to the rescue. Every family will find it easier to beat the credit crunch if they use just a few of the tips from this excellent book.

Adrian Coles
Director-General,
The Building Societies Association

Introduction

Money makes the world go round, so the saying goes. But, if money oils the wheels that turn the globe, by the same token a lack of money makes the gears seize up. Our happily spinning financial system has been slowed right down for more than a year now, as a result of a nasty spanner in the works called the 'credit crunch'.

A 'credit crunch' is a sudden fall in the availability of loans – or credit. For the ordinary consumer this generally means difficulty in obtaining mortgage finance, bank loans and easy credit on plastic cards. But what the consumer is suffering now has it roots beyond these shores. If, as chaos theory has it, the fluttering of a butterfly's wings on one side of the planet can cause a tornado on the other side, then it is hardly surprising that, in a global financial marketplace, problems overseas can have far-reaching consequences here.

Where Did It All Start?

The origins of the current credit crunch are to be found in the United States, with the collapse of the 'sub-prime' mortgage market. Borrowers who had been lent money by the banks to buy homes, even though they were considered a poor credit risk, began to default on their loans when interest rates went up, and introductory 'teaser' rates, which had lured them into taking up the banks' tempting offers, came to an end.

Because these loans had been packaged into bundles and sold on to other banks, as part of the wheeling and dealing of the financial system, the effects of the defaults began to be felt throughout the banking world. Like ripples in a pond, alarm spread first within the US, and then overseas banks which had had dealings with the US banks also became affected. Soon everyone was reluctant to lend to anyone else in case they did not get their money back. The financial system began to grind to a halt.

At the same time commodity prices started to rise rapidly, driven by demand from booming markets in India and China. The price of petrol, food and other goods has soared in recent months, and central banks have been reluctant to cut interest rates as they struggle to stem surging inflation. This, along with the banks trying to protect their profit margins, has kept the rate of borrowing expensive.

Consequences

It's not just home loans and easy credit that are affected by a crunch. When banks hoard their cash and don't lend, money in the whole financial system becomes scarce. This can have a frightening knock-on effect. The price of money – interest rates – goes up and lenders pick and choose who they lend to. People who have patchy credit records find it more expensive to borrow, if they can manage to borrow at all. House buyers can't get mortgages, would-be sellers can't sell because of the scarcity of buyers, and house prices fall. The value of some people's homes sinks below the amount of money they have borrowed on the mortgage – which leaves them in the dreaded 'negative equity'. They are then unable to move house to find a better-paying job, or to sell to release themselves from the mortgage burden, without being saddled with a massive debt.

Without access to credit, companies are unable to invest or take on new staff. If their customers or suppliers are unable to get credit, they may default on their payments, so companies start to fail and jobs are lost.

Northern Rock has been the highest-profile victim of the credit crunch so far. Instead of mainly using the money it had taken in from savers to lend out again to home-buyers in the form of mortgages, as many banks and building societies do, Northern Rock borrowed most of the money it lent out from other banks. When other banks stopped lending to it, the Rock's

business model collapsed and it had to be rescued by the Government to protect the interests of depositors and mortgage borrowers.

The Individual

So, what does the credit crunch mean for you? If you aren't trying to buy a house, you may think you aren't affected by it. But you would be mistaken.

On a personal level, even if you don't need finance to buy a house, you may find it hard to obtain car finance, a personal loan or a credit card, or you may discover that the cost of doing so has gone up sharply.

If the economic climate worsens, you may find your pay fails to keep pace with inflation, as companies try to cut costs. You may even find yourself being laid off or made redundant. While you may be able to take advantage of some temporary bargains, as failing shops sell off surplus stock or even close down, you may also be powerless in the face of other rising prices, such as fuel bills, and the soaring costs of transport and housing, particularly mortgages. Suddenly you need to cut back on your spending just to make ends meet.

And it is not just the low paid and those on fixed incomes, such as pensioners, who feel the pinch. A study by the insurance company Axa found that three out of four families with an income of more than £30,000 were preparing to cut their spending this year to cope with rising household costs.

While studies suggest that many people feel that they have not yet been affected too badly by the credit crunch, these people may begin to feel the strain if the crunch worsens.

What Can You Do?

A survey in *The Times* revealed that 66 per cent of those asked felt that their family would fare badly over the next year, while 77 per cent felt the country as a whole would suffer. While these views are probably justified – the Governor of the Bank of England is already hinting that Britain is on the brink of recession – there is still a lot that you can do to lessen the impact of the credit crunch.

Cutting spending doesn't necessarily mean cutting back. The key to beating the credit crunch is to make the money that you have go further, and to be smart with your spending.

That is where this book comes in. We show you how to make your money work harder for you by using a few tips and tricks that will cost you little or nothing and keep your wallet healthy.

Whether it's using a cashback shopping site, or taking the roof rack off your car to save petrol, using free software for your computer or collecting Marks & Spencer vouchers by taking your old M&S clothes to Oxfam, we show you how to beat the squeeze.

How This Book Will Help You

In the following chapters we tell you all you need to know about making the most of your money.

In the first section we help you to get your finances back in order, from reviewing your mortgage, changing your credit cards – or even cutting them up – and getting the best from your bank account.

You are never going to stop shopping, but the credit crunch shopper pauses before purchase and thinks carefully before splashing the cash. We show you how to make your hard-earned money go further – essential if you find yourself cash-strapped because of higher household bills. Check out the discount stores, buy second-hand and use price comparison sites to spend less and get more.

Necessities

One of the things we can't do without is food. Yet we can cut down on spending *and* actually eat a better diet with just a little forethought. Cutting out the cappuccino and buying more vegetables are just two money-saving ideas out of a host of recommendations to boost your bank balance while still enjoying what you eat. Don't worry, it's not all lentils and cabbage soup! We have suggestions for saving money in restaurants, too.

We also show you how to save on household bills by switching supplier, getting the best mobile deal and 'saying no to 0870', that horrid super-cost phone number beloved of customer helplines.

Travel, Leisure and Making Money

One area where you can certainly cut down spending is motoring. Of course you can always walk or take the bus, but if you do have to use the car, it's not just what you drive but how you drive. We tell you how to save money just by taking the junk out of your boot and paying for your fuel with a cashback credit card.

Holidays and leisure activities don't have to be expensive. We've some ideas about where to go on holiday and what to do to save your cash. But did you know that just changing the way you book, and even the time of day that you book, can save you money? We've also some ideas on saving money on sports and days out.

Finally, as well as saving money, we show you how make money from home to supplement your household income, and suggest some handy gift ideas that will please your friends and family but won't bankrupt you.

Happy crunch-busting!

Annie Shaw, Laura Howard and Simon Read
The CashQuestions Team

Personal Finance

The Importance of Personal Finance

Getting your personal finance arrangements right is probably the most central aspect of surviving a crunch on credit. Each one of your financial pots plays a big part in how much money you have left in your pocket after payday. This means that – whether it's mortgages, credit cards or even savings – if you are not on the best deal, you're going to lose out.

What Can You Do?

The days when consumers hopped casually from one deal to another are over.
As the credit crunch continues to bite, lenders are keeping their cash close to their chests and selecting borrowers with great scrutiny.

Seek Advice

Closer scrutiny and stricter criteria make it more important than ever to tread carefully towards the best deal and understand what you are buying – a combination that could well involve seeking out independent financial advice. You can find an adviser near you at www.unbiased.co.uk.

Take Steps

In the meantime, there is a plenty you can be doing, such as moving your savings to the right type of account that pays the best rate and getting on the starting blocks in plenty of time for your remortgage. You may even find yourself putting your credit card in a block of ice ...

Your Home

The short supply of mortgages as a result of the credit crunch has had two main effects. First, an increasing number of would-be first-time buyers are being rejected for mortgages beacuse banks and building societies have tightened their lending criteria. Secondly, existing homeowners whose mortgage deals are coming to an end are facing higher repayments as the cost of lending has gone up. And you may not even be close to being able to get a mortgage or buy, and instead will be renting, often at astronomical prices.

Mortgages

So whichever mortgage camp you fall into, how can you minimize the effect of the credit crunch when it comes to funding your own home?

Save

Regardless of the twists and turns of the economy, it's always been the case that the bigger deposit you can muster together when buying your first home, the better. This is because mortgage lenders want to lend to responsible borrowers who pose as little risk as possible. In their eyes, the fact that you

have saved is proof of this. Lenders also feel that, if a borrower has a stake in the property too, they will be less likely to default on the part of the home they have a mortgage against.

Bigger deposits: Since the availability of mortgage funding started to disappear as a result of the credit crunch, lenders are insisting on even bigger deposits, which means first-time buyers will have to save even harder. According to research from the information service www.mform.co.uk, mortgage lenders required an average 15 per cent deposit in 2007, but this has risen to a staggering 23 per cent of the property value in 2008.

Benefits: Having a more substantial deposit will suit you as well as the mortgage lender. Not only will you have a lower debt secured against your home, but you will also have access to a wider variety of different mortgage lenders and to deals with lower interest rates.

Meet Your Credit Report

Your credit report holds years' worth of information about your borrowing history and is therefore a good indicator of how reliable you are when it comes to repaying your debt. When you apply for a loan, a lender will look at this file to decide whether to agree the loan. It figures then that, during a credit crunch, your credit file is of more importance than ever.

How to see your credit report: Credit files are held (but not determined) by credit reference agencies; Experian, Equifax and Callcredit. You can apply online, on the phone or by post from any of these agencies for as little as £2. Or you can opt for a 30-day free trial of online access to your credit report at www.experian.co.uk.

Get on the Inside of Lenders' Sums

A little insight into how mortgage lenders do their sums can go a long way. Although the credit crunch has meant that 100-per-cent mortgages (which do not require a deposit) are no longer available, if you are debt-free, you can maximize your borrowing capacity by using a lender that employs affordability criteria rather than straightforward income multiples. This means that the lender will consider your monthly outgoings to calculate what you can afford to repay each month rather than just multiplying your salary by a certain amount. If your outgoings are low, you will be able to borrow more. Lenders that work on this basis include Standard Life and Abbey.

Use a Mortgage Broker

The credit crunch has made it very difficult for the uninitiated to find the right lender and mortgage deal for their circumstances, in which case a good mortgage broker or independent financial adviser (IFA) can be invaluable. There are some mortgage brokers that do not charge consumers, taking the fee from the mortgage lender they introduce your business to instead.

But bear in mind that they will still need to be paid from somewhere, so this cost will probably be factored into your mortgage. Even if you already have a mortgage and are coming to the end of your deal, lending criteria will have changed since the last time you applied. A mortgage broker can steer you through the credit crunch to find you the next best thing.

Plan Ahead

If you know that your mortgage deal is going to expire soon, you can bet your bottom dollar that your next deal is going to be more expensive. Mortgage interest rates have risen considerably in the past year, and the days of cheap lending are over – for now. In this case, take a run up to the problem, rather than waiting for it to hit you. Most lenders allow you to 'book' a rate from their current range of mortgages up to three months in advance of your remortgage, at no charge and without tying you into the deal. This means that if rates drop again, you can abandon what you have booked and opt for a different deal. Or you can up sticks and change lenders altogether ...

Don't Be Loyal

Even if you have been with the same lender for years, if it will no longer offer you the cheapest mortgage deal, make the jump to a competitor that will. However, make sure that any charges you incur to switch – such as exit fees to leave your old lender and administration fees to join your new lender – make sense to pay when set against the interest you will save by switching.

Pay More Now for Flexibility Later

It's important to bear in mind that your stated monthly mortgage repayment is a minimum and that most lenders allow penalty-free overpayments on the proviso they do not exceed 10 per cent of the original mortgage debt each year. While things may feel financially tight already, if you can pour just a little extra money into your repayments now, you will be rewarded with flexibility later on if things get tighter still. For example, you may be able to underpay to the level at which you have overpaid – or at the very least your lender will look more kindly on your case if you start to struggle further down the line. Overpaying on your mortgage will also reduce the chances of falling into negative equity, where the value of the house is less than the debt against it, should house prices continue to fall.

Don't Stick Your Head in the Sand

According to figures from the Council of Mortgage Lenders, approximately 1.4 million homeowners came to the end of cheap fixed-rate mortgage deals in 2008 and were faced with a monthly payment shock as they were put onto a more expensive deal. If you fall into this category and are struggling to keep up with your 'new look' repayments, ensure that you contact your lender as soon as possible and explain the situation. If one thing's for certain, it's that sticking your head in the sand will only make things worse in the long term.

Michael Coogan, director general of the Council of Mortgage Lenders, issued a warning about this recently. He said, 'The first step for anyone struggling to pay their mortgage is to contact their lender and get advice. Lenders will treat you fairly and use repossession only as a last resort. If you take positive action to contact your lender, pay what you can, and show up to court and make your case, you are more likely to reach an agreement with your lender that allows you to stay in your home. But you cannot just walk away and assume you are no longer responsible for the mortgage.'

Make a Temporary Switch to Interest-Only

You can reduce your monthly payments in the short term by switching to an interest-only deal. This means that, rather than paying the capital and interest with what's called a 'repayment mortgage', you ignore the capital of the loan and just pay the interest due to the lender. On a £200,000 mortgage taken over 25 years priced at 6.5%, this would see your monthly repayment fall from £1,350 to £1,083. However, while your monthly outgoings will be reduced by £267, this should not be considered as a 'saving'. The original capital sum will stay the same and the longer it takes to pay off, the more interest will be charged on it. Therefore, paying just the interest will cost you more in the long term – but in the short term, it could be a big relief.

Extend the Term of Your Mortgage

Continuing to repay the capital and interest on your mortgage, but extending the term, will also reduce your monthly repayment. For example, the same £1,350 payable on a £200,000 repayment mortgage taken over 25 years would cost £1,264 if it was taken over 30 years. But again, this should not be considered a saving because paying any debt over a longer period will result in more interest.

Take a Payment Break

If you are not entitled to a mortgage holiday, you may still be granted one if you can prove to your lender that your money troubles are only temporary. For example, perhaps you are in line for a pay increase or one partner is returning to work again after having a baby. In this case, your mortgage lender may agree to defer any interest payments – which, at the start of a loan, account for most of the repayments – for a short period and to treat the arrears as part of the original debt.

Seek Independent Advice

If your money worries are serious, it's a good idea to seek unbiased and independent advice. There are many organizations that you can turn to including Citizens Advice, Shelter, National Debtline and the Consumer Credit Counselling Service. Their debt advisers can assess your situation and devise the best course of action for you. See a list of further useful websites and phone numbers at the end of this section.

Rent Out a Room

According to research from Abbey Mortgages, more than 18.2 million homeowners have at least one uninhabited spare bedroom which, at an average monthly asking price of £289 per month, could generate an extra £3,468 a year – a sum that could easily tide you over the

credit crunch. In addition, the government allows each homeowner to receive up to £4,250 tax-free gross rental income a year under its Rent-a-Room scheme, which means that most people would not even pay tax on this income. Director of Abbey Mortgages, Phil Cliff, commented: 'With income being squeezed in so many ways, those looking to raise some extra money may find that freeing up their spare room could provide the answer.'

Beware of Sale-and-Rent-Back Schemes

'Sale and rent back' is the name given to a type of scheme that will buy your property if you are financially struggling – then rent it back out to you. In stress-fuelled times of a credit crunch, this can seem appealing at first glance, as a homeowner can remain living in the property, albeit as a tenant, which spares you the emotional turmoil of quitting a family or marital home. It will also mean that you can avoid the trauma of repossession or even putting your home up for sale in a market that smacks of tumbleweed. Sale-and-rent-back scheme providers also claim that you can get your hands on the cash quickly.

But sale-and-rent-back schemes are dangerous territory no matter how serious your money worries. Not only will you take a big hit on the amount that you are paid for your home, but also the industry is not regulated by the Financial Services Authority. This means that there are lots of cowboys out there who, as the new landlord of your home, could turf you out on the street anyway.

Consider Equity Release

If you are aged 50 or over, and find that, while your property is worth more than you ever imagined, you are struggling with the rising costs of day-to-day living, you may want to consider an equity release scheme. This means handing over part of your home to a specialist provider in exchange for cash or an income stream. The most popular way of doing this is with a lifetime mortgage, which involves taking a loan against the value of part of your home. A fixed interest on the debt rolls up until the house is sold when you die or move into care.

Reassurance: Under trade body SHIP (Safe Home Income Plan) rules, the final amount owed is guaranteed never to exceed the value of your home at the time – even if it has fallen.

Discuss: It is crucial to speak to your family before carrying out an equity release scheme, as it means that there will be considerably less in the 'inheritance pot'. For a list of providers of equity release, look at www.ship-ltd.org; for unbiased specialist advice, contact Key Retirement Solutions at www.keyrs.co.uk.

Homebuying Tips

House prices have dropped around 10 per cent in the past year as mortgage availability has dwindled alongside confidence in the housing market. In the summer of 2008, the Royal Institution of Chartered Surveyors (RICS) reported the quietest property market for more than 30 years. Growing families, job relocations and simply the usual course of life will still mean that people need to buy and sell homes – it is just that you may need a few tricks up your sleeve first.

Consider Buying Only Part of a House

According to mortgage information service www.mform.co.uk, first-time buyers need an income of £41,600 just to get a mortgage for an average property. If you don't earn this much, consider buying only part of a property instead under one of the government's shared-ownership schemes. This means that you have to qualify for only a proportion of the property value (between 25 per cent and 75 per cent) and the shortfall is stumped up by a local housing association. A manageable rent is then paid to the housing association on the part of the property you don't own. In the past, the government's shared-ownership schemes have been set aside predominantly for key workers, such as police officers, nurses and teachers. But now the schemes have been extended to anyone who wants to buy, but is not financially able. For more information and to see if you would qualify, visit www.housingcorp.gov.uk and click on Home Buy.

Pair up with a Friend ... or Two

Buying with a friend or sibling is a practical and pretty risk-free way of getting on the housing ladder during the credit crunch. Not only will two salaries boost your borrowing potential, but the cost of the mortgage and escalating household bills will be cut as well. You could even pair up with more than one friend; most lenders allow up to four individuals to be included on one mortgage agreement, but typically they will take only the highest two salaries into account for the mortgage.

Bear in mind, though, that when you come to sell any equity gained will be distributed according to the portion each agreed. Ask a solicitor or property lawyer to draw up a Deed of Trust – a promissory note that sets down ownership and payment responsibilities. You should also ensure that you are recorded as 'tenants in common' as opposed to 'joint tenants' and that anyone whose name is on the mortgage is aware that he or she is 'jointly and severally liable' for the entire loan – regardless of who's paid for what.

Exploit the Downturn in the New-Build Sector

Housebuilders and developers have been hit hard by the credit crunch, laying off staff and shutting their doors altogether. This means that they are being forced into offering incentives to first-time buyers that are definitely worth a look. This includes their paying for stamp duty, legal fees and even moving costs for first-timers, or providing a loan for 25 per cent of the property, which can be repaid over 10 years. But be careful where you buy. A glut of new-build apartments in some UK city centres has seen the value of this type of property plummet, pushing owners into a state of negative equity. Do some thorough research first.

Negotiate Hard on Price

The number of buyers registered on estate agents' books has plummeted in the past few years. As the summer of 2008 was drawing to a close, the average estate agent had just 226 potential buyers registered on its books, according to the National Association of Estate Agents (NAEA). This compares to a staggering 620 average at the same time in 2003 when the housing boom was in full swing. But less choice for vendors means that buyers are equipped with stronger bargaining tools with which to negotiate on price. So, while it always pays to play fair, don't be shy about some tough negotiating on the asking price. The seller can always say no.

Take a Credit-Crunch Compromise

Mammoth mortgages and easy borrowing have both stopped dead in their tracks as the credit crunch has taken hold. But in many ways this is not a bad thing. The most traditional way of bringing a home into the realms of affordability was to compromise. This might mean buying in cheaper neighbouring town, opting for fewer bedrooms or having a further 10 minutes to walk to the station in the morning – none of which is insurmountable.

Stay off the Ladder and Rent

With house prices continuing to fall and mortgage funding not being any easier to come by, there is a whole raft of would-be first-time buyers opting for a 'wait and see' approach. But everyone needs somewhere to live and – unless you have a generous family with a large house – this can usually result only in renting. However, the credit crunch has had a bearing on the cost of landlords' mortgages too, which has resulted in an increase in the average rent. According to a survey from buy-to-let lender Paragon, average monthly rents in the UK surpassed £1,000 for the first time ever in April 2008. But you don't have to take the price on the table. This is a tough market for everyone in the property business, and your bargaining powers can be put to good use when it comes to renting a property too.

Homeselling Tips

Selling your property in the deadest market since the 1970s is not going to be easy. According to property portal Rightmove, at the end of the 2008 summer, there was only one successful sale for every 15 homes on the market. This compared to one home in every seven on the market during the same time period in the previous year. In other words, selling your home is twice as difficult. But as well as adhering to the 'three Ps' rule of price, presentation and promotion, get the following cost-saving tips under your belt to make life easier:

Go Cheap on the HIP

Since 2007 every seller must, by law, have commissioned a Home Information Pack (HIP) before they market their property for sale. These controversial packs add anything between £300 and £400 to the already expensive cost of moving home. Given the fact that most buyers never ask to see the HIP, there is little point opting for the most expensive. Compare prices and providers at trade body the Association of Home Information Pack Providers (AHIPP). You can find them at www.ahipp.org.uk.

Buy Your HIP Upfront

HIPs are almost always cheaper to buy upfront as opposed to taking out an effective finance agreement that allows you to pay when the house is sold. Opting for these 'pay later' arrangements can also tie you into using that particular agent, which is not a good idea in such a difficult market. And remember, whether the house sells or not, you will have to pay for the pack anyway. If you do this when you 'de-instruct' the agent and take your home off the market, your pack is also likely to cost in the region of £100 more.

Negotiate with Your Estate Agent

Estate agents are one of the worst-hit industries during the credit crunch, as the lack of mortgage availability and increase in uncertainty have seen sales fall through the floor. In this case, one thing you can be sure of is that they will want your business. So rather than just accepting their initial quote, knock them down to a percentage or two. Don't feel too bad about it – although we all need to earn a living, the agent will soon tell you if the instruction is not worth their while.

Don't Spend a Fortune on Decorations

In the current housing market, you are unlikely to make a return on any major home improvements. So rather than spending £10,000 on a new bathroom, you would be better off buying a few tins of neutral paint and freshening up each room. This won't add value either, but it might make your property more appealing and entice a potential buyer to come back for a second viewing.

Extend Your Home Instead

It's not just a bigger mortgage that is going to hurt the pocket if you move up the property ladder. The cost of stamp duty, legal fees and removals is going to be pretty hefty too. So why not stay put and build on? You may still need to borrow, but at least the outlay will be going back into your home rather than to outside parties. According to recent research from insurer LV=, almost 1.5 million homes will undergo or have plans draws up for new extensions over the course of the next 12 months rather than being sold as a direct result of the credit crunch.

Credit Cards

Credit cards can be an excellent servant, but a terrible master. For example, if you make a large purchase (of more than £100) with a credit card, you will automatically be protected by section 75 of the Consumer Credit Act. This means that if the goods fail to arrive or are damaged you can pursue the lender as well as the retailer for breach of contract. Another benefit is that, providing you pay off your balance every month, you can actually make money from some credit cards. This is because you won't pay a penny in interest and special 'cashback' credit cards offer as much as five per cent of what you spend on the card back in your account every year.

Take Control to Avoid the Pitfalls

On the other hand, when you are not in control of your credit cards, things can work out to be very expensive – for example, if you have one or more outstanding balances on high-interest cards on which you are making only the minimum repayment. In times of a credit crunch, the first rule is to clear debts, starting with the most expensive – and this means taking a firm hand with your credit card.

Check the APR

As the credit crunch has taken hold, a number of credit card issuers have been hiking up the annual percentage rate (APR) that applies after the initial attractive 0 per cent introductory period – as they are perfectly legally entitled to do. But, according to price comparison site Moneysupermarket, more than one in four cardholders (27 per cent) didn't know if the APR on their card had increased in the past 12 months. The first port of call then is to check with your credit card provider(s) to see what rate of interest you are being charged – it could be a lot more than you think.

Switch to a 0 Per Cent Credit Card

If you do have an outstanding balance that is generating sky-high interest, look at transferring it to a card that charges 0 per cent interest on that sum. There are several on the market – see www.moneyfacts.co.uk for a list. Bear in mind, however, that the balance won't be charged at 0 per cent for ever – usually between 10 and 12 months maximum. Note also that new purchases made will be charged at the card's APR. These days, credit-card providers will also charge you a balance transfer fee in the region of three per cent. So if you want to transfer £5,000, for example, you will be charged £150. But as the £5,000 will then generate no interest for a set period, it's usually worth taking the hit.

Choose a Fair Credit-Card Provider

Don't look solely at the interest rate when switching to a new credit card, as there will be other factors to build into its long-term economic efficiency.

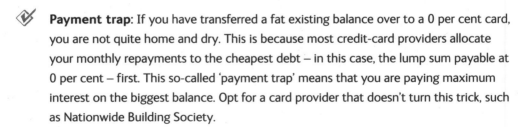

- **Payment trap**: If you have transferred a fat existing balance over to a 0 per cent card, you are not quite home and dry. This is because most credit-card providers allocate your monthly repayments to the cheapest debt – in this case, the lump sum payable at 0 per cent – first. This so-called 'payment trap' means that you are paying maximum interest on the biggest balance. Opt for a card provider that doesn't turn this trick, such as Nationwide Building Society.

- **Foreign charges**: Similarly, if you are jetting off on holiday and intend to use your credit card abroad, look for one with no foreign charges – available from Nationwide Building Society, the Post Office, or Abbey.

Good Credit-Card Practice

Be Kind to Your Credit Rating

The days when consumers held the power, flitting from one credit card to the next and transferring large balances as they went, are over. Post-credit crunch, card providers are less inclined to accept your business in the first place. This is why your credit file is of paramount importance. Make sure that you pay all other financial commitments on time, whether it's a mobile phone bill, council tax or catalogue purchases, to give yourself access to the cheapest cards.

Pay Your Credit-Card Bill on Time

Paying your existing credit card on time is also crucial in retaining a healthy credit file. It will also mean avoiding a frustrating situation whereby penalty charges are added to the total bill, increasing your debt further. The best way to make sure you pay on time is to set up a monthly direct debit from your current account.

Always Pay More than the Minimum

Paying your card provider's minimum repayment – typically around two per cent or £5, whichever is the greater – will mean you end up going round in circles when it comes to clearing your capital balance. For example, on a credit card balance of £1,500, if you only ever pay the minimum monthly requirement of two per cent of your outstanding balance, the bill will take more than 30 years to clear and cost thousands of pounds in interest. A better approach is to pay back the maximum you can afford each month, meaning you pay less overall interest and are shot of the debt sooner.

Start Paying off What You Spend Every Month

In addition to making inroads on eroding the balance of your credit cards, get into the habit of paying off whatever you spend on the card at the end of each month. This way, you know that, whatever happens, your credit-card debt is not getting any bigger. Better still, leave the card at home and, where you can, use good old-fashioned cash.

Cutting down Credit-Card Use

Put the Spending on Ice

If the relationship you have with your credit card is unhealthy and you can't trust yourself to use it just in emergencies, put it in a tub of water and freeze it. This way, if you feel an impulsive purchase coming on, you'll have to wait for it to thaw out.

Cut the Card up

Consumers spent an overwhelming £4.4bn less on their credit cards in the first half of 2008 than during the same period last year, according to research conducted by customer insight specialist G2 Data Dynamics – a clear indicator that people are preparing for darker days. If you can't stop spending on your card, take a pair of scissors to it, which will leave you just with the reality of the bill.

Opt for a Pre-Paid Credit Card

The credit crunch has deemed perfectly legitimate borrowers unable to obtain a credit card. If you are among them, a pre-paid card, where money is loaded on in advance, could be the answer. Not only is there no risk of running into debt, but also you will not undergo credit checks or pay interest on any 'outstanding balance'. However, currently these cards are not cheap to run. Over-the-counter purchases carry a fixed charge of between 99p and £2, or a fee of up to three per cent could be applied to each purchase.

Loans

Loans of any description have been harder to come by since the credit crunch and, in any case, they are almost certainly always best avoided. However, there are some things in life for which you simply have no choice but to borrow. In this case, make sure that you have chosen the cheapest and most flexible personal loan available.

How to Get the Best Deal

Shop around for the Best Rate

With the cost of borrowing going up, it's more important than ever to shop around for your loan rather than simply accepting what your bank offers you. The cheapest personal loans are usually available online, where you are not indirectly paying for the overheads incurred by running a branch network and employing thousands of staff. But even before you opt for one of these, look at a loan comparison such as like www.gocompare.com to compare rates.

Don't Make Too Many Loan Applications

Make sure that you are clear about which loan to go for before you make any application. If you make too many loan applications – especially if they have been turned down – you will leave a 'footprint' on your credit file which will make subsequent lenders less willing to accept you.

Be Flexible

Just as with with your mortgage, overpaying on any loan will mean you pay less interest and are debt-free quicker. But not all personal loans will allow overpayment. Ensure that your loan is flexible, which means it will not charge you a penalty to either overpay or clear the debt should you come into a windfall or receive an inheritance during the term of the loan.

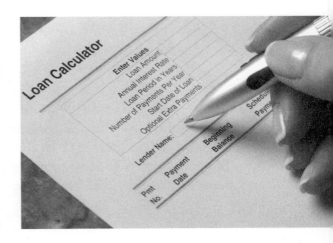

What to Avoid

Secured Finance

Make sure that you avoid taking a secured loan if you can possibly help it. Secured loans are otherwise known as 'second-charge mortgages'. This means that, just as with your primary mortgage, if you can't service repayments your home is at risk and could be repossessed. Your mortgage lender will be paid off first, then whatever's left will go to the second-charge lender. Because secured loans are available for up to 25 years, compared with a maximum of around 10 years on an unsecured loan, repayments are lower so that they can seem like a good way to consolidate your debt or fund a large purchase such as a new car or even a trip around the world. But, even though secured loans are now regulated by the Consumer Credit Act, you are still pinning your repayment on the roof over your head. And with falling house prices, this could also leave you in a state of negative equity. By contrast, with an unsecured – or personal – loan the worst that can happen if you default on payments is that you damage your credit file.

Steer Clear of Forecourt Finance

Research from comparison site www.uswitch.com from September 2008 (a month in which 20 per cent of all new cars are purchased) found that motorists were set to throw away £168 million by opting for car-dealer finance rather than hunting down the cheapest personal loan. Taking this route instead of giving into the car salesman's dealership finance could save an average of £826 each in interest payments over three years, the research found.

Insurance

In an ideal world, we could all afford to be insured up to the hilt for any and every eventuality. But we don't live in an ideal world, and a credit crunch makes it less ideal still. In this case, one way of freeing up your monthly outgoings is to look carefully at what insurance policies you have and check that they are all necessary.

What Is Necessary?

It can be difficult to work out what is necessary and what is surplus to requirements. These few points may help you on the way.

Don't Create a False Economy

Cutting out some insurance policies could, at best, be a false economy and, at worst, an unspeakable life trauma. For example, to suddenly stop paying for your buildings and contents insurance as other costs take priority in the credit crunch would of course invalidate your cover. This means if your home burned to the ground or was ruined by a flood, you would be left with the bill – as well as the mortgage – regardless of the reduced value of the property. Saving a few pounds on some insurance policies can be a false economy too. For example, there is no point paying £10 less for your travel insurance policy, only to find that, when you come to claim, it is littered with exclusions and you are left out of pocket and unprotected.

Consider the Real Worth of Your Life

If you are a young single homeowner with no dependants and struggling to make ends meet, there will be more useful places for your money than life insurance premiums – such as

keeping up with your mortgage and household bills while you are still alive! If you are a couple living together, perhaps consider taking out life insurance for the highest earner or take a joint policy whereby payment is received on the first death. However, if you have a family, life insurance is a must. When a member of your family dies unexpectedly, the last thing you'll want to think about is working more hours, the cost of childcare or even selling your home.

Getting the Best Deal

Get the Best Motor Insurance Deal

Every year when it comes round to renewing your motor insurance, it always feels as if you are too busy to compare alternatives. But a quick check on a comparison site such as www.gocompare.com may reveal how much you could be saving on your car insurance for what is effectively the same service.

Up Your Voluntary Excess Payment

The higher the excess you are willing to pay, the lower your premium will be. Pushing up your excess can save up to 20 per cent with some insurance products – something that many providers omit from their sales pitch.

Pay Premiums Annually

The vast majority of us pay for our home and motor insurance monthly without thinking about it. But most insurers charge a steep annual interest rate for the privilege, which can easily add up to another £100 a year. While it may seem like a blow at the time, paying upfront for insurance such as home and contents, motor and pet will save you money in the long run – not to mention free up your monthly outgoings through the course of the year, which will help you to budget. And if you save throughout the year to foot the bill, you'll gain interest on the balance too.

Policies to Avoid

Some insurance policies can more confidently be argued as unnecessary. Take a look at the following.

Don't Pay for a Policy That Won't Pay

One kind of insurance policy that often comes under fire is mortgage payment protection insurance (MPPI). This is a 'one price fits all' insurance which charges per £100 of cover – a typical rate is about £5 per £100. This means that, if your mortgage repayment is £1,000, MPPI will cost you a hefty £50 a month. But, according to recent figures from the Office of Fair Trading, a meagre 15 per cent of claims are paid out. This is because MPPI typically excludes pre-existing conditions as well as new conditions if they are stress- or back-related. Even if you do qualify for a claim, MPPI will pay out only for a year, and this is usually after an initial deferment or 'excess' period of between 30 and 60 days. In this case, providing you are young and fit, income protection can be a cheaper and more comprehensive alternative.

Axe the PPI

When you are taking a loan, credit card or any kind of finance, you are bound to be asked how you would service the repayments if you lost your job, fell ill or had an accident. The representative will then try to sell you payment protection insurance (PPI) as a solution. Not only are these policies notorious for not paying, but most of the time they are not necessary as well. If you put aside some of your own money every month for this eventuality, you will soon be able to cover a few months' repayments – and gain the interest on the balance if you don't.

Decline Phone Protection

Similarly, think before signing up to mobile-phone insurance, as it is rarely worthwhile. A policy can add £5 to £10 a month to your bill and should cover you if your phone is lost or stolen, and any fraudulent calls made. However, a replacement handset can usually be bought for very little outlay, and it's probably covered by your home contents insurance anyway.

Say No to Extended Warranties

Extended warranties are another retailing trick designed to make you part with more of your cash than you intended at the point of purchase. These contracts are sold over the counter – typically when you buy electrical home appliances, such as a fridge or washing machine. They offer a continuation of the

standard manufacturer's guarantee of the product – which typically lasts for 12 months – for a further, say, three or five years. But recent tests carried out by consumer watchdog Which? showed that most modern appliances were unlikely to break down in the first few years after purchase. And even if they do, consumers could be protected under the Sale of Goods Act, which says goods should be of 'satisfactory quality' and last a 'reasonable' amount of time.

 Buy an extended warranty elsewhere: Nevertheless, if a warranty makes you feel better, you don't have to buy one at the shop where you bought the item. There are a number of firms – including insurance companies and the manufacturers themselves – that sell extended warranties that can be cheaper and more comprehensive than one from the retailer.

Budget

According to the dictionary, one meaning of the word 'budget' is an 'estimate of income and spending for a set period of time'. But, while some people have always been better at this than others, the cheap and easy access to borrowing that consumers have become accustomed to in recent years has meant that people have felt it less necessary to budget than they did in other generations. The credit crunch is a stark reminder that budgeting is essential – regardless of your income or age.

Cutting out Spending

Before you have even allocated a budget for what you need to spend, check that you are not throwing money away on unnecessary items.

Give Standing Orders and Direct Debits a Spring-Clean

Before you draw up a workable budget, take a look at a list of your standing orders and direct debits online, or call your bank to get the information. Often there are expenses lurking in there that are no longer relevant or necessary, but you have been paying regardless. For example, when is the last time you used the gym that you are shelling out £50 a month for, and do you ever have time to watch the DVDs you subscribe to religiously every month? Perhaps your current account now applies charges and you could stop these by simply opening another account with the same bank. Cutting out unnecessary spending such as this will make your finances feel lighter – which is a great way to start your new credit-crunch budget.

Reduce Unnecessary Daily Spending

When you look at your day-to-day life carefully and what's really necessary to spend, making savings should be easy. For example, just by forfeiting your daily takeaway coffee, you will feel richer by the end of just one week. If you are a regular smoker, kicking the habit can save more than £5 a day. And when it comes to Saturday night, why not open a bottle of wine, cook a special dinner and make use of the home you work so hard to pay for? Using a bicycle, especially in the summer months, will see you fitter as well as save on petrol and parking costs.

Supplementing Your Budget

As well as reducing the money leaving your account, try to increase the money going in. This doesn't have to mean taking on an evening job or holding your boss to ransom unless you get a pay rise. See also the section on Making Money from Home (page 224).

Claim All Benefits Due

By spending five minutes filling in some basic details about yourself, your pay and your status, you can find out if you are entitled to any government benefits by logging onto www.entitledto.co.uk. The site, which is free and funded by the sales of software to local authorities and other organizations, will list all the tax credits and benefits you could and should be claiming. Well worth a look considering the amount going unclaimed.

Claim Back Bank Charges

If you have paid overdraft charges in the past six years, you may be able to claim them all back. There is a hold on the claims being processed at the moment, but there's nothing to stop you from applying anyway. Find out the amount you are claiming first, download a template letter from www.moneysavingexpert.com and send it to your bank.

Get Overpaid Tax Back

No one likes giving anything to the taxman, and the usual way to deal with this reality is to put your finger over the gross figure earned when you receive your monthly pay slip. However, in doing so you may have missed the fact, that you have been paying too much tax for years and are due a windfall. To find out if you are owed by the taxman, visit www.hmrc.gov.uk and click on Claim Back Tax.

Reunite with Your Money

Finding a £5 note in your coat pocket from last year is always a bonus, but there could be more cash with your name on it lurking in the past. Let the credit crunch spur you on to carry out some simple detective work surrounding dormant or even childhood accounts. The website www.mylostaccount.org.uk helps you to track down money in all kinds of forgotten nooks and crannies. For lost pensions, investments, insurance policies and old share certificates, try the Unclaimed Assets Register at www.uar.co.uk.

Sell Your Clutter

According to a recent survey by car manufacturer Chevrolet, a staggering 1.1 million additional traders attended boot fairs this summer to sell their clutter and feather their nest against the credit crunch. Chevrolet also found that the average revenue generated by a seller at a boot fair is £142, while a typical household claims to have £870 worth of unused goods. So for an investment of between £5 and £10 for a pitch for your car and an early Sunday morning start, turning your clutter into cash should also give your new budget a kick-start.

Coping with Budgeting

Be Realistic

Once you have minimized outgoings and maximized incomings, you should be in the right frame of mind to start working on your budget. But, just like drawing up a rigorous exercise plan, compiling a budget is easy. It's the sticking to it that's hard. So be realistic and factor in the odd glass of wine, meal out or weekend away.

Don't Give up

Once you have been operating your budget successfully for a few weeks, remind yourself that your weekly spend is a limit – not a target. If you find that there are any other measures you can take to reduce your daily, weekly or monthly spend, carry them out immediately. The less money that leaves your current account, the more comfy your nest will be against the cold winds of the credit crunch.

Enjoy It

Budgeting needn't be depressing. In fact, according to a recent 'emotion survey' by online greeting card service www.greetz.co.uk, 38 per cent of the population said they were actually enjoying a return to a 'less materialistic' way of life brought on by having less money to spend.

Savings

Regular saving is a very good habit at any point in time, but midway through a credit crunch it makes more sense than ever. First, banks are tripping over themselves to get money in, rather than lend money out, which results in staunch competition and higher and higher savings rates. What's more, having freed up more cash in your current account through drawing up a budget and spending less in response to the credit crunch, saving should be easier than ever. Lastly, having some savings that you can 'pull out of the hat' at any point during the credit crunch will mean that you can sleep easier at night.

Maximizing Interest

Make sure that your savings account is working as hard as it can to make the best of your money by ensuring that you accumulate as much interest as possible.

Utilize Your Tax-Free Allowance

The first place to start saving your hard-earned cash is in an ISA (individual savings account) where the taxman can't get his hands on the interest earned. As you would expect from any tax incentive scheme, the government has placed a cap on the amount you can put into your ISA each year. From 6 April 2008, this cap was increased to £7,000 to £7,200. A maximum of £3,600 of this annual allowance can be saved in cash, while the remainder can be invested into a stocks and shares ISA held with the same or a different provider. Alternatively, you can choose to save less in cash and more in stocks and shares – or simply invest the entire £7,200 in a stocks and shares ISA.

Secure the Best Rate

Regardless of the type of account your savings are held in, you will want to ensure that they are earning the best rate of interest possible. With record-high savings rates a silver lining of the credit crunch, shopping around for the best rate should be fun. Look at www.moneyfacts.co.uk for the best market rates.

Keep Interest Earned Ahead of Inflation

One longer term problem with saving in a credit crunch is that high inflation, as we have seen in the past few months, means your 'rainy day' money is worth less in real terms. So to ensure your savings are fighting against the general cost of living, consider an inflation-beating account from the likes of National Savings & Investments (NS&I) or Leeds Building Society.

What Type of Account?

It pays to look beyond just the rate and to the type of savings account.

Minimum Deposit

If you open a regular savings account, you will have to pay in a minimum sum each month. If this minimum is unrealistic, you will incur some kind of penalty. This could be a reduced interest rate or loss of an annual bonus, or the account may be closed altogether.

Instant Access

If a minimum deposit is not for you, you may be better off with an instant access savings account, even if it pays a slightly lower rate of interest.

Understand Savings Protection

The collapse of Northern Rock blew a hole in the confidence of consumers when it came to the security of their hard-earned savings. But for most people, most of this is psychological. From 1 October 2007, the Chancellor Alastair Darling increased the limit at which savings are guaranteed under the government's Financial Services Compensation Scheme (FSCS). Now a maximum of £35,000 will be protected in the event that a bank is made insolvent, or £70,000 for people with joint accounts. Where you have accounts with different brands or subsidiaries of one company, your compensation will be limited to a total £35,000.

Investments

The pockets of many investors have suffered a serious blow in the past year as the share prices of banks on their backs has steadily fallen. Even share prices within the traditionally most reliable sectors, such as food and telecoms, have fallen as a result of the credit crunch, as big companies in the sector – one after another – announced poor sets of results.

Stay out of the Market

If you are a totally inexperienced investor who has come into some cash from a windfall, inheritance or even a redundancy, consider putting the sum into reducing your mortgage debt rather than investing in stocks and shares. The waters are still murky out there, and navigating them for the first time would not be so worrying if you had paid down your debt first.

Do's

If you want to take the plunge, you would do well to take heed of the following.

Tread Carefully

Even more experienced investors should take a cautious approach to new investments in times of economic uncertainty. Many experts say that a 'drip-feed' approach of gradually investing money in stocks and shares is the best way forward. This way you are not missing out, and you can't lose too heavily either.

Keep a Balanced Investment Portfolio

Diversifying your investments (in other words, not putting all your eggs in one basket) is always solid and reliable advice – and the reason why is obvious. If one of the stocks in a diversified portfolio suffers a large loss, the impact on the overall portfolio is likely to be very small. If, however, that stock represents a significant percentage of the portfolio, the loss could be devastating. In the credit crunch, where losses are so stark, this age-old golden nugget of advice should be taken to heart more than ever.

Don'ts

Don't Invest in Anything You Don't Understand

This is a good lesson in any economic climate, but is often revisited when share prices plunge. While you cannot predict the movements of your investments, make sure that you at least have a thorough understanding of what you are investing in. It takes more than a gamble to build a successful investment portfolio.

Don't Assume It's a Bargain

In the past year, one silver lining of the credit crunch on investments is that shares are cheap. But if they are not selling, they are clearly still not cheap enough to encourage investors to start piling their cash back in. Just as with being attracted by a brightly coloured 'sale' tag in a shop, when you would not have looked twice at the item when it was at full price, step back and take a wider view of any 'cheap' shares before putting down your cash.

Don't Be Swayed by Dividends

Everyone likes getting their hands on 'here-and-now cash', and dividends of investments pay out even when share prices are falling. However, even companies paying the highest dividends have taken a severe kicking in terms of their share price. Be very careful not to confuse the two.

Advice and Solutions

If no amount of credit-crunch tips is going to help, and you feel really worried about your debt levels, the best thing you can do is to act. These days, worried consumers have access to free, unbiased and non-judgmental organizations that will listen to your problems in confidence without trying to sell you things. Try the following contacts for advice, and check out the potential solutions that they may suggest detailed at the end of the section.

Organizations

A variety of organizations exist to help you with your debt or housing crises. Here are some examples.

Citizens Advice Bureau

The Citizen's Advice Bureau (CAB) will point you in the right direction if your debts are spiralling out of control. Visit www.citizensadvice.org.uk or make an appointment at your local branch.

National Debtline

This organization is experienced in listening to consumers' debt problems and will offer free and independent advice. Visit www.nationaldebtline.co.uk or call 0808 808 4000.

The Consumer Credit Counselling Service

This is a registered charity that offers free counselling and debt advice and 'can help you get back in control of your money and on with your life'. Visit www.cccs.co.uk or call free on 0800 138 1111 to speak to a debt counsellor.

Credit Action

This is a national money education charity that will help you with your debts. Visit www.creditaction.org.uk or call free on 0800 138 1111.

Shelter

This well-known organization is not just a charity for the homeless – it works to prevent homelessness too. If you are worried about losing your home, contact them at www.shelter.org.uk or call on 0808 800 4444.

Online Advice

If you are simply feeling the pinch and looking for the best way to turn in a tightening credit environment, there is a whole host of online help. See these useful websites:

- **www.cashquestions.com**: This website is owned and run by a panel of personal finance journalists and independent financial experts. If you register and ask any personal finance-related question, you will get an unbiased answer free of charge.

- **www.moneysavingexpert.com**: Money-saving expert Martin Lewis's website of the same name has been hailed as the king of economy websites. It has a huge raft of money-saving tips which can be sent directly into your e-mail inbox.

- **www.uswitch.com**: If you are looking to reduce the costs of your gas and electricity bills, uSwitch.com makes the process quick and easy.

- **www.financialadvice.co.uk**: This website offers the latest financial news and advice on the best deals in pensions, savings, investing and all money matters.

✓ **www.moneymatterstome.co.uk**: If you are starting or expanding a family during the credit crunch, then this website could be useful. It provides a practical guide to family finance whatever form your family takes.

✓ **www.whataboutmoney.co.uk**: A useful site for 16- to 24-year-olds that clearly sets down how much money buys you what – and how many hours you have to work to get it.

✓ **www.moneysupermarket.com**: This giant cost-comparison website allows consumers to compare the best deals on all financial products from loans to insurance and mortgages.

✓ **www.gocompare.com**: A transparent and easy-to-use cost-comparison site that will find the cheapest insurance deals – but tailored to your specific needs.

✓ **www.childtrustfund.gov.uk**: Children born on or after 1 September 2002 receive a £250 voucher from the government with which their parents can open a Child Trust Fund for when each child turns 18. This website gives details of how to choose the right account.

Know Your Solutions

It may be that talking to an expert is all you need to motivate you to turn and face your debt demons head-on. But, if you can't manage on your own, there are several options available to you. Knowing what they are in advance can make the whole process less painful.

A Reduced Payment

The first option to exhaust is reaching an arrangement with your creditors yourself. Call each one direct, explain your situation and see if you can come up with a new repayment schedule. This may result in the interest being frozen for a set time and added on to the capital, or extending the term of the debt to make it more manageable. Don't be afraid to call your creditors – they will be polite and appreciative that you have made contact. And there are two things of which you can be certain: they will want to work with you to get their money back, and they will have heard a lot worse before.

A Debt Management Plan (DMP)

When the sums just don't add up, you may qualify for a debt management plan. This allows borrowers to make one-off smaller repayments each month to a charity such as Credit Action that will, in turn, distribute the funds among creditors in proportions agreed in advance. A DMP is often the best option as it does not deem an individual insolvent.

An Individual Voluntary Agreement (IVA)

If a DMP is not agreed you may qualify for an IVA. This is an agreement between a borrower and his or her creditors which is drawn up by an IVA provider and sets down an affordable set monthly payment over a five-year period. In order for the IVA to be accepted, 75 per cent of creditors (by value, not number) must approve the proposal. The IVA must also be agreed by an insolvency practitioner (IP) who is regulated by one of seven professional bodies, including the Insolvency Service and the Law Society. However, IVA providers themselves are not regulated. After the IVA term – providing you have met the terms and conditions – you will theoretically be debt-free. However, most IVA plans now require a proportion of the equity in your home is given up at the end of the plan. Evidence of the IVA will also remain on your credit file for up to six years.

Bankruptcy

Declaring bankruptcy is stressful and upsetting but, if debts are out of all proportion to your ability to repay them, it could be the only option. Bankruptcy means that you lose control of all your assets – most notably your home – and you are unable to obtain credit or act as a company director. Evidence of the bankruptcy, even after it has been discharged, will stay on your credit file for up to six years. However, despite the stark disadvantages that bankruptcy brings, many people still feel a sense of relief; they no longer have to worry about servicing impossible repayments every month and at least have a clean financial slate in their sights.

Shopping

Shopping Rules

Shopping is not called 'retail therapy' for nothing. Treating oneself to a new pair of shoes or a new shirt can cheer up an otherwise dull day. But spending without thinking is off the agenda for the credit-crunch-conscious.

Shop Savvy Not Shabby

You will do well to adhere to these two rules when shopping in general. One of the keys to budget shopping is psychological preparation.

Don't Stint on Quality

The first rule of credit-crunch shopping is that you don't have to sacrifice quality when money-saving. In fact, the savvy credit-crunch shopper seeks out quality, but simply pays less for it. But you may have to change your habits and throw your prejudices out of the window – and that includes shopping online if you don't do so already, buying second-hand, using discount supermarkets and switching branded goods for cheaper generic items.

Pause Before You Purchase

The second rule is that you must resist impulse buys. Impulse buys mean that you often acquire things you don't need or never use. The 'no impulse buys' rule doesn't mean 'no treats'. It means only buying things you really want, and planning where to buy them, to make sure you buy only things that are going to be really useful or treasured, and you pay the lowest price that you need to. This involves planning your shopping strategy. So, what weapons can you gather for your credit-crunch armoury?

Sales Shopping Best Practice

You probably already visit high-street sales in the big multiple stores. But don't be blinded by the array of potential bargains on display and dive in headfirst.

Golden Rules

An otherwise lovely item in a hideous colour or the wrong size is a waste of money, even if it only cost you a penny. The must-follow rules of sales shopping are:

 Do you really want it?: Buy an item only if you would have bought it anyway, if money were no object.

 Will you use it?: It's not a bargain if you don't use it or wear it.

Beware Meaningless Sales Spiel

'Up to 20 per cent off' is pretty meaningless when you don't how many of the goods are at this discount. Also, '100 extra points with this item' might look like a big discount because 100 is a big number, but how much is one point worth?

Look out for Bargains among Shop-damaged Goods

During sales, items often have a tag indicating damage and the reason for the reduction. If you find more damage elsewhere, ask for a further reduction – remember, there is no harm in asking. Examples of damage are:

- **Stains:** For instance, a top that has been pulled over someone's head and become smeared with makeup is probably a good buy, as one wash with some biological detergent will have it as good as new again. Watch out for 'dry clean only' labels, though. You could end up paying more for the dry cleaning than for the soiled item if it needs professional cleaning.

- **Buttons:** Items with missing buttons can be good buys too, as long as you can replace the button easily or move fancy buttons round, so that if you have to replace the missing one with an odd one it won't show.

- **Zips:** Clothes with broken zips are generally not a good buy unless you are an accomplished home sewer. Even then you will need to deduct the cost of buying a zip from your potential saving. If you need to have the zip professionally replaced, the item is less likely to be a bargain.

Buy Gifts in Advance

Christmas comes only once a year, but it always seems to take shoppers by surprise. If you always keep Christmas in mind, you can buy your Christmas gifts throughout the year, snapping up bargains in sales. Some of the best bargains to be had are in the post-Christmas sales themselves. This is the time to buy wrapping paper, Christmas cards and anything non-perishable that you can use next year. The same goes for birthdays and wedding gifts. Plan to suit your pocket, and don't overpay because you have left it too late.

Take Care with Electrical Goods

When choosing larger electrical goods, don't just plump for the lowest price. You need to take energy efficiency into account too. A cheap freezer or washing machine could eat up the value of its cheaper price in energy costs – and repairs, if it's unreliable. Use a guide such as the ocnsumer magazine *Which?* to find the best buys. If you don't want to take out a subscription, it is often available in public libraries.

Go for Energy Efficiency

If you decide to buy a new electrical appliance, look for the Energy Saving Recommended logo – a blue wedge – which indicates an efficient appliance that will be cheaper to run. With energy prices soaring, you are even more likely to save money in the long run by paying a little more for a more efficient model now and using less power.

White's All Right

When buying large electrical goods such as fridges and washing machines, choose white. Items in other colours can cost more than £50 above the price of an identical item in white.

Cash in on Clearance Items

Comet holds auctions of clearance items at cut prices. Go to www.clearance-comet.co.uk for new, end-of-line, refurbished and damaged items.

Discount and Low-Cost Shopping

There's more on the discount stores in the Food section of this book (pages 98–123), but these shops can be excellent for other items too – from electrical goods to clothing and cosmetics. Then there are the more familiar low-cost shops, outlet shopping and many other ways of achieving discounts on your purchases.

Supermarket Shopping

If you look beyond the big-name supermarkets, it's surprising what you can find. The credit crunch has seen a surge in the fortunes of the low-cost supermarkets, such as Aldi, Lidl and Netto. Once the haunts of pensioners and people on lower incomes, these budget stores are now attracting middle-class shoppers, who are deserting Sainsbury's and Waitrose in droves to fill their baskets more cheaply.

Non-Food Products

Aldi regularly offers high-spec computers at amazingly low prices. It also has televisions and other goods, such as housewares and DIY equipment. Lidl offers excellent electrical goods and computer peripherals, as well as clothing and household items. Netto sells everything from DVD players to babies' cots. All the discounters sell cheap cosmetics and household cleaning materials.

Range v. Quality

The range at the no-frills stores may be more limited than you are accustomed to, but the quality is surprisingly good, and the savings that can be made mean that it is worth taking the trouble to seek them out.

Evidence of Quality

The following examples show how you can genuinely expect quality products at good-value prices:

 Skin cream: In a study by Channel 4's *How to Look Good Naked* show, which asked 100 women to blind test a range of popular face creams, Aldi's Siana Skin Kind Nourishing Anti-Wrinkle Night Cream was voted the joint best skincare product, together with luxury brand Lancôme's night cream. The Aldi product cost £1.89, while Lancôme's cost £51 a pot – 27 times more. Aldi's day cream, costing the same as the night cream, was similarly voted best anti-ageing product in its category.

 Lavatory paper: *Which?* magazine recently published a study which found the luxury brand Andrex Quilts to be the best lavatory paper, with a score of 89 per cent. Velvet Quilted came second, with 79 per cent, but Lidl's Floralys came neck and neck with Waitrose's Quilted Ultra Soft with a score of 78 per cent, well ahead of other Andrex and Velvet brand products and own-brand supermarket toilet tissue. The leading Andrex product, however, costs 0.34p per sheet compared with just 0.21p for the Lidl product, a massive 61 per cent difference in price for a barely perceptible difference in quality.

Shampoo: *Chat* magazine said of Aldi's Giani Calvaro Professional Shampoo and Conditioner: 'Looks expensive, but it ain't! At just 99p per item, with sleek packaging and salon formulas, these shampoos and conditioners are everything the hairdresser ordered to bring your hair back to life.'

Get in Early

Remember, however, with regard to the budget retailers that, although the core food, cleaning materials and cosmetics ranges remain reasonably stable, household items, clothing and electrical goods are stocked on a 'WIGIG' basis – when it's gone, it's gone. Advance notice of special offers is published in in-store leaflets and online, so you can get a preview of when something particularly interesting is coming up, but you can't just walk into the store and be assured of buying a cheap computer or set of bath towels, as you can in other mainstream stores that stock a wider range.

Other Cheap Stores

It is probably unnecessary to belabour the point that bargains can be had at the likes of Primark for clothing and linens, and Ikea for furniture and household items – if you can stand the queues – but anyone trying to save money who hasn't visited these stores and their imitators will be amazed at the low prices compared with the major high-street retailers. Outlet shopping is another option.

Try the Obvious

Primark is stocking stylish winter coats from just £25 this season. A wide mixed-stone bracelet costs just £2.50, with a matching ring costing £1.50. Colourful bath towels cost £4. You can buy a bed frame at Ikea for just £27 and a roller blind for £4.99. H&M, UNIQLO, Peacocks and Bonmarché are other budget clothing brands that you might not usually buy, but you can certainly supplement your wardrobe with a few T-shirts or tights, if nothing else.

Outlet Shopping

This can be a source of great bargains, depending on what you are looking for. For housewares they are great, but for clothing and shoes you might have to settle for last season's fashions. Sports goods are a good buy. Manufacturers such as Nike are constantly updating their range, and the aficionados love to have the latest gear, but ordinary mortals who just need a pair of crosstrainers for going to the gym can enjoy cut prices on last season's lines.

Money-Off Vouchers

Look out for vouchers when reading magazines and newspapers. These may be for money off retail purchases or 'two-for-one' offers at restaurant chains, giving two meals for the price of one at certain times. Some of these deals are so good that you will often find it is worthwhile buying the newspaper or magazine simply to get the vouchers, even if you never read the publication and put it straight in the recycling.

Haggle

The credit crunch has made retailers ever more anxious for sales. Not only do they have their ordinary sales targets to meet, but also, when the worst comes to the worst, they need to clear their old stock to make way for new, and many sales personnel will go to quite extravagant lengths to make a sale. This gives you your chance to haggle.

Choose Your Target

Obviously, trying to haggle over the latest Nintendo Wii or Apple iPhone is going to get you nowhere when there is a waiting list of potential buyers standing in line behind you. But when it comes to the old version of a piece of electronic equipment, or last season's clothing, which needs to be moved before the new stock can come in, it's another story altogether. A product that was a best buy last year but has been superseded by a newer model is still going to be a good-quality product – but you can probably now get it for a song because most people are more interested in the newer model.

Buy a Bundle, Get One Free

There are various tactics you can adopt. Among the easiest is to buy a bundle of items and ask for one of them free. A typical scenario would be buying a new computer and asking for a free printer or broadband router. You might buy some expensive kitchen equipment – say, a range cooker – and ask for an extractor hood free. If you are buying furniture – a sofa, say – ask the store for some free cushions to accompany it.

Find a Fault

The next tactic is to find a small fault with the goods – presumably you wouldn't want them if the fault was severe. You could ask for shop-soiled or damaged goods at a discount. This is a good tactic if you think that the shop needs to shift its stock quickly, or when trying to negotiate over bulky items such as furniture, which take up a lot of room on the shop floor.

Pay Cash, Get a Discount

If goods have an offer with 'interest-free credit', that's the equivalent of a price discount, as the buyer does not have to hand over the money until the free period is over and can notionally earn interest in a savings account on that same money. Turn the offer on its head if you can afford to buy the item outright, and ask for a discount if you pay in cash. A starting point would be a discount equivalent to the total amount of interest being waived if you had taken up the interest-free offer.

No Credit Card, Get a Discount

Unlike online retailers, many high-street stores charge the same amount for goods however you pay for them, as part of their marketing policy. Smaller personally owned stores will be acutely aware that accepting a credit card costs them a high percentage of the transaction price in merchant's fees. Ask for a discount if you pay another way — by cheque, debit card or with cash, for instance.

Personal Care

Personal care is an area often forgotten about when trying to cut spending, but you can keep the price of personal care down if you shop around for over-the-counter medicines and for eyewear.

Medicines

Don't Buy Branded Medicines

Save money by buying non-branded items such as aspirin rather than Anadin, ibuprofen rather than Nurofen, and ibuprofen gel rather than Ibuleve. In other words, any medicine sold under a trademark name that is available without a prescription probably has an own-brand or generic equivalent. When you are looking for medical items, look on the ingredients panel on the product you were going to buy, then look for a similar unbranded item with the same ingredients. For example, a blister pack of branded paracetamol-based painkillers for treating a headache can cost as much as £1.48. A same-sized item containing the same ingredients and sold without a trademark name from a discount store costs 16p, albeit in less fancy packaging.

Pre-Pay Prescriptions

Prescriptions are now free for residents of Wales, and have been reduced in price to £5 in Scotland, prior to the abolition of prescription charges in 2011. Currently, though, residents of England and Northern Ireland have to pay (£7.10 at the time of writing) – although Northern Ireland residents have had their prices frozen at the time of writing and may see charges waived in future. If you need frequent prescriptions, it could be worth applying for a pre-pay certificate or 'season ticket'. A four-month certificate costs £27.85 and a 12-month certificate costs £102.50, and you can pay for the 12-month one in 10 monthly instalments. If you need five or more prescriptions over four months, or you need 15 or more in a year, you will find using a season ticket cheaper than paying each time you go to the chemist. You can apply for a pre-payment certificate by using the form that you can download from www.ppa.org.uk, or you may buy one from a pharmacy registered to sell the certificates. You can also call 0845 850 0030 to purchase a certificate; have your debit card or bank details handy, as you will need to give them when you order your certificate.

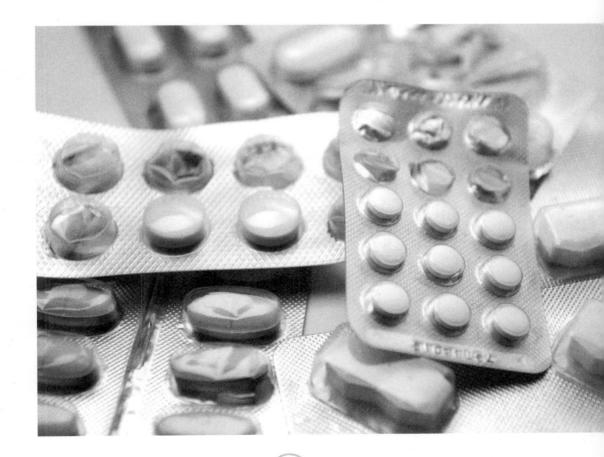

Buy Drugs over the Counter

You may also be able to save money on prescribed drugs. If a doctor prescribes a medicine but it is one that is available without prescription, it may in some cases be better for you to purchase it yourself rather than have the pharmacist complete the prescription. Some pharmacies, including Boots, will tell you if it is advantageous for you to buy the medicine yourself. With others you may need to ask the dispensing pharmacist about the comparative prices. Always follow the doctor's directions if you purchase for yourself an item that has been prescribed for you. In some cases, these directions may vary from the directions printed on the packet because of a special need that you have. If you have any doubts about dosage or method of administration, check with your doctor or the pharmacist.

Buy Online

Another way to buy non-prescription items and save money is to buy from a website such as www.chemistdirect.co.uk. The site guarantees lowest prices and delivery is free. Although it is possible to buy prescription drugs online, usually from abroad, this is not recommended, as you should take prescription drugs only under the direction of your doctor. If you buy from abroad, you have no guarantees about the source of the medicine, whether it is a genuine product or counterfeit, how the medicine has been stored since it was manufactured or the condition in which it has been kept during transit.

Eyecare

Glasses and Lenses

Glasses and lenses can work out to be very expensive if you have a complicated prescription and want fancy designer frames or lenses, but if you need just basic frames you can get glasses as cheap as £10 from websites such as www.specsonthenet.com or www.budgetspex.com. Frames from www.GlassesDirect.co.uk, www.Spex4less.com and www.goggles4u.com are a bit more expensive. Buying glasses online is not for everyone, as the opportunity for seeing if the frames suit you is limited. Although the online services will use your prescription to endeavour to make the glasses exactly right for you, fine adjustments won't be possible, as they would be at an optician's shop, and refunds may be possible only if the supplier makes a glaring error and not if your failure to supply vital information renders the glasses useless. If you want to take a chance, however, the savings can be considerable.

See yourself: Some sites let you upload a photograph of yourself and 'try on' the glasses online.

Pick-up service: Tesco website www.tescoopticians.com offers an online order service, and you can pick up your glasses in-store.

Buy Contact Lenses Online

You can't really go wrong with buying contact lenses online, as what you buy on the Net is the same product that you buy in the shop. The market is keen, so shop around. Websites to check out if you wear standard lenses include www.getlenses.com, www.postoptics.co.uk, www.tescoopticians.com and many others. For one-day Acuvue lenses, check out www.secondsightonline.co.uk or www.contactsuniverse.com.

Play Your Cards Right

There are all kinds of loyalty, credit and store cards around, some of which can save you money, while others might cost you dear unless you use them carefully and judiciously.

Loyalty Cards

Many high-street stores, including supermarkets, bookshops, health and beauty outlets and even coffee shops, offer loyalty schemes. Many of these use a plastic card that looks like a credit card or store card (but is not the same thing), so that it can make a record of your spending habits and tailor its marketing to you. Some people object to this 'spy in the wallet', but for those who don't mind loyalty schemes can give great savings. The schemes usually give you points which can be exchanged for money off your shopping.

Updates

If you sign up for e-mail updates or newsletters as well, you receive notice of special offers and often get money-off offers addressed specifically to you, especially if you haven't used the card for a while, as an encouragement to go back to the retailer.

Boots Advantage

Among the best-value loyalty cards is the Boots Advantage scheme, which gives you four points for every £1 you spend – so it is effectively a four per cent discount on your future shopping.

Tesco Deals

Sometimes shops exchange the points you accumulate for vouchers with a face value of more than the cash/shopping alternative. For instance, if you redeem your Tesco Clubcard points vouchers via the Clubcard Deals brochure, you can get deals worth up to four times the face value of the vouchers. Typical offers include a year's subscription to *Company* magazine for just £6 (normal price £24), RAC membership for £27.75 (normal price £111) or a ticket for Alton Towers for £8.75 (normal price on the gate £35).

John Lewis

The John Lewis card, which is a credit card rather than just a loyalty card, gives you one point for every £1 spent at John Lewis, Waitrose and Ocado, and £2 spent everywhere else (since it is a credit card), which can be spent at John Lewis outlets.

Cashback Cards

In much the same way that the cashback websites share their commission with you the shopper, credit-card companies will pay you to use their card when you shop. Several leading-name credit cards offer you cash or points depending on how much you spend.

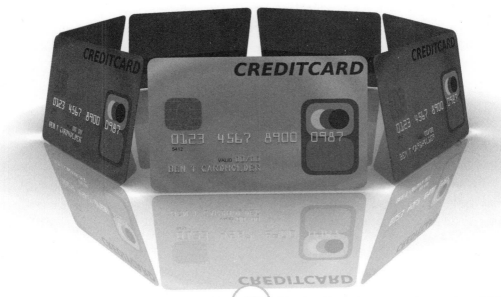

American Express

The most generous card at the time of writing is the American Express Platinum MoneyBack credit card, which gives you a huge five per cent cashback for the first three months on all your spending on the card, with a maximum rebate during the period of £200, then 1.5 per cent cashback after that, uncapped.

More Leading Examples

Other leading cashback cards are Barclaycard's Cashback card, paying four per cent for the first three months, capped at £15 per month, then 0.5 per cent thereafter; Citi's Shell MasterCard, which gives you three per cent off Shell fuel and a one per cent rebate on purchases elsewhere; the Egg Money card (not to be confused with the ordinary Egg card), which also pays one per cent cashback, but additionally offers Egg Rewards, giving discounts off purchases made with the card; and Capital One's Low-Rate Credit Card with Cashback, which offers a less generous 0.5 per cent cashback on every purchase you make.

Vital Rule

But a word of warning: using a cashback card is only for people who pay their bill in full every month. Cashback cards tend to charge a higher rate of interest than many other cards; if you can't afford to pay off what you have spent each month, you would be better off with a card charging a lower interest rate – which will save you far more than you could earn in cashback to compensate for a higher rate.

0 Per Cent Purchase Cards

These include the Capital One Platinum card, the Halifax One Online Special, the Tesco Bonus credit card and the Mint card from Royal Bank of Scotland. These cards don't ask you to pay back the money you owe, apart from a minimum monthly payment required by all card issuers, for a period as long as 14 months.

Beware

These cards save you money only if you stash the cash you would have used to pay the bill in a high-interest account, then pay the bill at the end of the free period. If you don't put money aside to make the full repayment when it is required, you are going to be hit with a very expensive credit-card bill, running at between 12.9 and 15.9 per cent annual interest – a much more expensive way of paying than stumping up the cash or meeting your bills as you go along.

Store Cards

These are the cards that individual stores or store groups offer. They work like a credit card, but you can use them only in the particular store or group that they apply to. Store cards are a danger zone because of the high interest rates many of them charge. For anyone liable to succumb to temptation they are best avoided. There are, however, a couple of reasons for the disciplined, savvy shopper to take out a store card.

The Initial Discount

Many store cards lure you in with a massive discount on your first purchase. In this case, take out the card, use the discount, pay the bill in full when asked to do so and cut up the card, without spending anything else on it. Then use a cashback credit card for future purchases at that store (see the section on cashback cards, pages 79–80).

Club Benefits

The second reason to have a store card is that holders often become members of a privilege club, which gives access to special sale days, a free catalogue or other benefits. Once again, if you have signed up for these benefits, that is fine, but then dump the card.

Online Shopping

You can still manage to buy the same products as before simply by switching your shopping to online. You can buy everything from clothes and CDs to furniture and household goods online, with items often cheaper than their equivalent on the high street. Virtual discounters such as the Amazon book site or www.cdwow.com and www.play.com mean that books, CDs and DVDs can cost just two-thirds of the price of those sold in earthbound stores. Online shopping also means that you can choose goods from retailers who don't have a physical presence in your area.

Technology Is Your Friend

You need look no further than here for some great general tips on getting the best from your online shopping adventures.

Widen Your Horizons

With online shopping, you can even buy from abroad. When, in the realms of the trend-conscious, Crocs shoes and Ugg boots were all the rage and UK stores were sold out, canny UK shoppers bought their shoes from Taylor Shoes (www.taylorshoes.com) in Kansas City and Hartings (www.hartings.co.nz) in New Zealand, where stock was not only available, but also cheaper than the UK even when postage was taken into account. But do beware customs duties.

Use a 'Shopbot'

To make sure you find the cheapest UK retailer, use a 'shopbot'. These are price-comparison websites that trawl through lists of retail prices to find the cheapest for the item you want.

It is worth using at least three bot sites, such as www.kelkoo.co.uk, www.pricerunner.co.uk, www.pricegrabber.co.uk and www.shopping.com, as not all retailers have relationships with all of the shopbots, and you may not find exactly what you want if you use only one. As well as the general shopbots, there are also shopbots that deal with a particular market, such as DVDs or wine: for example, www.find-cd.co.uk; www.find-dvd.co.uk, www.bookbrain.co.uk, www.shopgenie.co.uk (for DVDs and books) and www.quaffersoffers.co.uk (for wines).

Rent, Don't Buy

Unless there is a particular title that you think you will want to watch over and over again, join a DVD rental scheme such as LoveFilm, Blockbuster and Tesco rental, and save both money and storage space in your home. Better still, hire DVDs and CDs from your local library for a few coppers. To save even more, watch free films online on BBC iPlayer and 4od, Channel 4's on-demand online service, which also offers a pay-per-film option.

Watch out for Credit-Card Charges

Retailers are allowed to charge an extra fee if you opt to pay by credit card, and even by some debit cards. The extra protection afforded by a credit card, as outlined above, can be valuable, but for trivial sums or transactions that you think are unlikely to be vulnerable to fraud, such as a hotel booking, use a debit card and save money on the credit-card surcharge.

Online Bargains, Discounts and Savings

Buying online is often automatically cheaper than the high street, but there are ways to bring the cost down even more.

Voucher Codes

You can often get a cheaper price by using an online promotional code. Find them at www.myvouchercodes.co.uk, www.hotukdeals.co.uk, www.shopcodes.co.uk and www.voucherheaven.com. The website www.sendmediscounts.co.uk also has information about promotional codes, shopping discounts and special offers online.

Get Cashback

Several websites now offer cashback on purchases. Many ordinary websites receive commission on sales resulting from responses to the advertising that appears on the sites. The cashback sites take this idea further and rebate some of this commission to the purchaser of the advertised service or item. There are many of these sites, but not all are equally reliable in making payments. Some are simply not worth the trouble of signing up. Still others may give a good service, but choose to give you shopping points instead of cash, or they make you reach a certain points total before they pay out, which may not suit you.

Rpoints and Quidco: Two of the most reputable sites are www.Rpoints.com, which promises to rebate to you up to 30 per cent of the purchase price at almost 2,000 online stores, and www.Quidco.com, which rebates 100 per cent of the commission to you and makes its money from the £5 subscription you pay to sign up. However, the £5 is deducted from the money you earn on the site – so if you end up not actually buying anything you pay nothing.

More: Other cashback sites include www.cashbackkings.com, www.greasypalm.co.uk and www.topcashback.co.uk. As with the shopbots, it may be worth checking out more than one of these, as not every site has a relationship with every retailer, and sites may have negotiated different deals with retailers for greater or smaller commission rates.

Some Bargain Websites

Here are just a few examples of useful websites for seeking out bargains:

ASOS: Fashionistas will love www.asos.com (As Seen On Screen), which finds you the latest designer looks at lower prices. To get a bargain outfit, all you need to do is type in a celebrity's name and you will be shown a lookalike outfit for not even half the price of its designer equivalent.

Deals Centre: Another site to look at is www.dealscentre.co.uk, which gives you information about online shopping deals, promotion offers and discount vouchers at companies such as Boden, Apple, the White Company and Dell.

Furniture: If you are looking for bargains in larger items such as furniture, try www.furnituredeal.co.uk and www.discountfurnituredirect.co.uk.

Shop Safely

There's no point in trying to save money only to lose it because you get ripped off, so make sure that you shop safely online.

Credit Cards

Using a credit card can give you protection under the Consumer Credit Act. If your goods are faulty or the shop fails to deliver them, the credit card company is obliged to refund your money, provided that the transaction is for more than £100 (although some will refund for smaller purchases). Holders of Visa debit cards can use the 'chargeback' scheme to get a refund. With chargeback (which is different from the credit-card scheme), there is no minimum or maximum limit on a claim, but the claim for a refund must be lodged within 120 days of the transaction. Chargeback applies only to Visa cards and not those in the Maestro group.

Secure Websites

If you shop online, you should use only sites that ensure your card details are kept secure. This means that the website uses technology that protects your bank details from online fraudsters and hackers. You'll know if it is a secure site if the website address begins with 'https' and if a small padlock icon appears in the bottom of your window.

Buy on eBay

The eBay website www.ebay.co.uk has come a long way from its roots as something of an online jumble sale. You can pick up many used and brand-new bargains from private and professional sellers, but, as with any trading environment, you need to watch out for scams and items for sale that aren't what they seem to be.

Set up a PayPal Account

The first step towards starting to buy is to set up a PayPal account, which lets you make instant online payments. It takes a few days, so make sure that you do it before you want to buy. A PayPal account is not essential, and you can often pay by cheque or postal order, but it has several benefits:

- **No limit on who you can buy from:** Many sellers prefer PayPal, and some will accept payment only by PayPal, so you will restrict the number of people you can buy from if you don't have a PayPal account.

- **Protection:** PayPal is owned by eBay and, although some people grumble about the expense of using the service, it does give you certain guarantees and protection in respect of eBay transactions, should a dispute arise.

- **Speed:** Using PayPal also gets your purchases to you more quickly, as payment is instant, so the seller can post off the goods as soon as practicable, without waiting for a cheque to clear.

Payment Methods to Avoid

Never, ever pay with cash or by telegraphic money transfer, such as Western Union and Moneygram. The ebay website itself has banned sellers from listing telegraphic transfer as a payment option, and if you enter into a private arrangement with a seller to pay this way you are completely unprotected. As the payment method is prohibited by eBay because it provides no safeguards for the buyer, you might well be suspicious about the seller's intentions if he or she suggests that you use it.

Watch out for Scams

While eBay takes measures to ensure fraud is kept to a minimum, with 84 million users worldwide selling goods to the value of £32 billion each year, it is an uphill task to keep the fraudsters out. Even though the company claims that 95 per cent of all fraudulent listings are removed from the site before the auction ends, it is still wise to take your own precautions because scamsters can and do slip through the net.

- **If something looks too good to be true, it probably is**: This particularly applies to designer labels being sold at suspiciously low prices. While eBay tries to ban anyone selling counterfeit goods from the site, and has strict rules on how items are described, it is not always successful.

- **Spotting fakes**: There are useful guides, both on eBay and elsewhere on the Net, on how to spot fakes. Just type 'how to spot a fake on eBay' into an internet search engine, and you will find plenty of information about what to look out for.

- **Suss out the seller**: When you are buying from a private seller, have a look at what else they are selling or what they have sold in the past. Does it look like a householder having a good clearout, or are they a professional dealer? Check their feedback – the reports left by other people who have had dealings with the seller – although you should always bear in mind that feedback can be manipulated, so it cannot be regarded as a 100-per-cent-reliable guide.

- **Ask questions**: A reputable seller will be happy to answer questions about a product and supply more information about an item, or even send you more photos of it. If the seller refuses to do this, you should be suspicious.

What to avoid: If you are an inexperienced buyer, don't buy from abroad, and don't buy expensive electronic goods (such as computers and mobile phones) or tickets for travel or concerts. These areas are rife with scams and are best left to experienced buyers who know what to look for. Start with low-value goods in private sales as you feel your way.

Work out Your Tactics

Don't bid too early in the sale – check what time it ends. Clever sellers put their bids in late, often just seconds before the sale ends. But be mindful that you may not be the only one employing this tactic, so you may be outbid before you get a chance to rebid – which is, of course, the idea.

Check Prices and Limit Yourself

Check the price of a similar item new. Many a bidder has become carried away and ended up paying more for a second-hand item than they could have paid for the same item in the high street. Remember to include the postage and packing charge when making your calculations. Decide how much you are prepared to pay, and don't go above that price.

Good Practice

When the sale is over, if you have won, pay promptly, and remember to leave feedback once you have received the goods.

Second-hand and Repair

Second-hand is good. As long as the item you have your eye on is serviceable and is something that would have been acceptable new, you are saving money – and you are saving the planet by keeping the item out of landfill. Think 'antique' – maybe more valuable than new. Think 'pre-loved' – an item that has been treasured and can be treasured again. Equally, think twice about throwing out perfectly good items just because they have a slight fault that could easily be repaired with a little effort.

Second-Hand is Not Necessarily Second-Best

Look at it this way: a new car loses a third of its value once it is driven off the garage forecourt. An average new car costing £15,430 to buy could lose up to 42 per cent of its value during the first year on the road, working out as a loss of £17 per day. If you advertised the car that you had just bought new for sale a week after you bought it, you would have to ask a lower price for it than the garage sold it to you – even though the car was as good as new. Most people will settle for a second-hand car, but many will then turn their nose up at used clothing or children's toys. But once you have worn a dress, or your children have taken a toy home from the shop, it *is* used – by you and your family. You would sleep in clean sheets slept in by another customer at a hotel, so why not wear an item of clothing that someone else has worn – as long as it has been properly laundered?

Charity Shops and Car-Boot Sales

Charity shops and car-boot sales are a bit hit-and-miss. Bargain hunters always have a quick look around to see if anything catches their eye. Only the unwise treat them with disdain and miss out. Since the arrival of websites such as eBay, where people can sell their unwanted items and get good prices, you are less likely to find hidden treasure than you would have been a few years ago – indeed, most charity shops use professional valuers to make sure a Rembrandt doesn't get sold for a song, and many charities also have their own eBay shops where they can offer the most attractive items to a wider audience (see shopping on eBay above).

But don't knock charity shops and car-boot sales. They are great for retro fashion and odd bits of china and glass. Anyone who has to equip a student's bedsit can do it cheaply from a charity shop, and goods will usually be of better quality than those bought brand-new from a pound shop. Many people use charity shops as a sort of public library, buying novels and other books there cheaply, then taking them back when they've read them.

 Hint: If you are a Marks & Spencer shopper, take your cast-off M&S clothes into Oxfam and receive a £5 M&S voucher to put towards a brand-new outfit.

Think Antique

Visit salerooms for second-hand furniture. For the best deals, look for really old items rather than nearly new. Pre-1950s sofas and armchairs will be properly upholstered, using traditional materials such as horsehair and kapok, rather than modern moulded foam, and will last a lifetime.

Gumtree

For larger local items, eBay's fellow site Gumtree (www.gumtree.com) can be useful. It carries all sorts of advertising, including flats to let, but also offers furniture and electrical items from people who just want rid of them cheaply.

Second-hand Music

For used CDs try www.musicmagpie.co.uk, which offers CDs at bargain prices – and sell your old CDs as well.

Refurbished Items

If you don't want to pay full price, consider buying a refurbished item. Many electrical manufacturers offer refurbished items either directly, via special micro-sites, or via eBay shops. The items are those that have been returned for some reason, have been repaired with genuine manufacturer's components and carry a full guarantee as though the product was bought new.

Swap Shops

You can still make something of your cast-offs by organizing swaps. Invite your friends to your house for a 'frock party', and ask them to bring along the clothes and accessories they no longer wear and swap them for something else.

Dress Agencies

These are the upmarket version of the second-hand clothing shop. Not only can you pick up top-of-the-range designer clothing for a fraction of the price, you can also sell your unwanted items to make extra cash. Dress agencies are emphatically not junk shops and are usually very picky about what they sell. They know their market and what is in fashion, and clothes are usually stocked for only a few weeks before they must be removed by the owner, or they are given to charity. Items must be in perfect condition. Find your local dress agency online, in the classified advertising section of your local newspaper or in the Yellow Pages. Dress agencies are ideal for finding something for a special occasion, such as a glamorous party or a wedding, when Primark just will not do. Members of the royal family have been known to pass unwanted items to dress agencies and – you never know – at the next wedding you go to you may see the mother of the bride wearing an ensemble that has once clad a royal personage.

Make Do and Mend

You can save money by making the best of what you already have, rather than just throwing it away and buying something else. You might even enjoy the experience!

Gok Your Frock

Take a tip from TV fashion star Gok Wan and customize a dress to bring it up to date by adding bows, belts and buttons, or slashing the hem line. Charity shops are ideal hunting grounds for buckles and buttons, bits of lace and scarves to dress up an old outfit.

Learn to Sew

A list of colleges offering sewing classes can be found on www.hotcourses.com. Look out for sewing classes at your local community centre or on the www.gumtree.com site for your area.

Running Repairs

Wear laddered tights under trousers. Recycle your boyfriend's old T-shirts as nighties. Mend handbag and briefcase straps with a guitar or camera strap, or even a dog lead – the best type is a chain 'coupler' used for walking two dogs at once that has a catch on each end, and is available from pet shops or eBay.

Re-cover Your Sofa

Don't buy new a IKEA sofa or armchairs. Instead, buy new covers for your old one from Bemz (www.bemz.com). You can cover an Ekeskog armchair for as little as £57.78. If you're not sure what colours you like, don't worry, the website lets you 'try out' different colour schemes by dragging and dropping the colours and patterns onto different IKEA furniture styles to see how they look.

Free and Easy

You can shop for free, if you know where to look. Well, not shop exactly, but you can pick up other people's unwanted items advertised on websites, send off for free samples, and get details of all sorts of free deals and outings. It's not too good to be true!

Websites

Free items available on websites are usually unsaleable or bulky, which people have difficulty getting rid of easily, but there can be rich pickings if you want things such as 100 flower pots to prick out your seedlings, a television for the spare room or bunk beds for visiting nephews. You will also find people trying to offload sacks of baby clothes and other baby items, which are ideal for credit-crunch-conscious new parents. Try the following:

FreeCycle

The website www.freecycle.org is a 'grassroots and entirely nonprofit movement of people who are giving (and getting) stuff for free in their own towns.' Their point is that 'it's all about reuse and keeping good stuff out of landfills.'

SwapitShop

The www.swapitshop.com website allows children to swap unwanted items, such as unsuitable gifts or outgrown collections, for other items.

A Portal to a World of Freebies

www.searchfreebies.co.uk tells you where you can get free stuff, such as a meal out, DVDs or phones. It also tells you where to get discounts and which shops have clearance sales. Other good sources of free offers are www.magicfreebiesuk.co.uk, www.freebielist.com and www.free-stuff.co.uk.

Send away for Free Samples

Many organizations offer you free samples, either in-store or online. This may be for the sake of market research – to ask your opinion of a new product, to spread the word about the product or to acquire your mailing details so that they can sell you other products. While you shouldn't just give away personal details to people you don't know, perfectly reputable companies such as Procter & Gamble, Nestlé and Boots offer samples. What you can get free is virtually endless, ranging from cosmetics samples to detergent sachets, tea and coffee, nappies, calendars and posters – you name it.

Free Software

You can find plenty of cheap computers on the internet, both brand-new and second-hand. New computers sold for home use tend to be loaded up with lots of software if you buy them from a traditional retailer. Computers sold for business use are often sold without programs and applications, and if you buy a second-hand computer you may find it has had its hard drive wiped clean. If you buy a computer that isn't fully equipped, you can save money by using free software.

Operating Systems

If you don't want to pay for an operating system such as Windows, download the open source (free to use) Linux or Ubuntu (www.ubuntu.com). If you don't want to use Microsoft Office for your word processing and spreadsheets, download Open Office from www.openoffice.org for producing documents. Incidentally, if you are looking for a bargain computer, the ASUS EEEPC 2GS-W001 2GB laptop costs just £159.58 including VAT from www.ebuyer.com. It has the Linux operating system and Open Office 2.0 already installed. The Acer Aspire One A110-Ab 8GB Netbook, with the Linpus Linux Lite operating system installed, costs just £219.99 from www.amazon.co.uk.

Anti-Virus Software

Even if you have bought a brand-new computer with Windows and Office already installed, you can benefit from free anti-virus software. Anti-virus software downloaded or bought on disk from the likes of Norton and McAfee can cost as much as £50, but equally good programs are available to download online free for personal use. Among the most popular anti-virus packages are Grisoft's AVG 8.0, Alwil Softaware's Avast! 4 and Alvira's Antivir. They can all be downloaded free of charge from www.download.com.

Avoid Conflicts with Free Trials

If you intend to use a free software program and you have a new computer, don't open up the free three-month trial that may be included with your program bundle. Simply delete it from the list of programs using the Add/Remove Programs tool. The free trial version is put there to encourage you to pay a subscription after the introductory period is over, and the program can sometimes prove tenacious and difficult to get rid of if you decide you don't want to continue to use it. As you should not run more than one anti-virus program at a time, if you want to use a free program you need to remove other programs completely to avoid the two sets of software conflicting with each other. Once you have your free software installed, remember to set the program to download frequent updates to make sure that you are adequately protected from new threats. New viruses appear on an ongoing basis, so your needs to be ongoing too.

Firewall Software

As well as anti-virus software, you will need a firewall. Windows provides a firewall, but it blocks only inbound threats. Having a firewall that blocks outbound threats can be useful, as it will tell you if you have accidentally picked up a virus and are attempting to transmit it. The most popular free firewall is probably Zone Alarm from Zonelabs, which can also be downloaded free from www.download.com. Make sure you download the 'free' version and not the 'free-trial' version, or you will be pestered for a subscription when the trial comes to an end. Remember to turn off your Windows firewall if you are using Zone Alarm because, as with anti-virus software, you should not run two firewall programs at the same time.

Food

Keeping down the Cost of Food

Food spending is one area where most of us could cut down. Whether it's dinner out or ready meals, a coffee before work or plastic-wrapped vegetables at the supermarket, it would be unusual to find a family where cuts could not be made to spending, while at the same time the quality of their meals was maintained or even improved.

According to the latest cost-of-living index, the annual increase in the cost of food has spiralled to a record 13.7 per cent, which means that families need to find another £1,400 a year to pay for the weekly contents of their shopping trolley. A basket of staple goods, including milk, butter, pasta, meat and bread, has jumped by 27 per cent over the past 12 months, as the effects of global food inflation wreak havoc on the UK diet. The price of wheat alone, which gives us bread and pasta, has climbed a horrific 130 per cent over last year's.

So How Can a Credit-Crunch Shopper Cope?

Cutting spending on food doesn't mean a diet of baked beans. It means that you need to plan your meals and think before you fill your supermarket trolley with expensive processed food. There are some basic measures to consider before you take more drastic steps.

Learn to Cook

The biggest money-saver is cooking nourishing food yourself. Simple meals, such as pasta dishes and soups, can be prepared in a trice at a fraction of the cost of ready meals – and, as you grow more confident, they are more delicious and more nutritious too. Remember, you don't have to be Gordon Ramsay to put together a simple meal. Invest in a second-hand copy of Delia's *How to Cook Book One*, or type 'learn to cook' into a Google search for some basic instructions. If you can read, you can cook.

Make Your Own Packed Lunch

Even if you're not up to boiling a panful of pasta, you can surely make a sandwich. According to research by the mortgage bank Alliance & Leicester, six out of ten people now regard as necessities things that were once considered luxuries, such as takeaway lunches or bottled water. They collectively spend more than £19 billion a year that could be spent elsewhere. Six and a half million people (14 per cent) buy lunch from a shop at least 'several times a week'. Making your own lunch can save you a fortune every week and, if you choose the right ingredients, it will be a healthier option too.

Avoid Vending Machines

Bring your own snacks and drinks to work. Crisps, confectionery and drinks cost much less from the supermarket, particularly if you buy in bulk.

Cut out the Cappuccino

Almost two million Brits buy takeaway hot drinks, such as a shop-bought latte, at least once a day. Cutting out the largest-sized latte at Coffee Republic, Costa Coffee or Starbucks each working day of the year would save you a cool £459.20. If you drink two shop-bought coffees a day, you could be doing serious damage to your waistline as well as your wallet – especially if you accompany them with a pastry or muffin. Remember, you are paying out of after-tax income. Give them up, and you are looking at the equivalent of a pay rise of more than £1,000.

Go Veggie

Cutting out meat once or twice a week can save you money. Consider butternut squash risotto instead of the old standard of spaghetti bolognese as an easy midweek dish.

Buy Loose Not Wrapped Fruit and Veg

The ready-wrapped produce is handy to pick up and throw in your trolley. It's ready-weighed and priced, but you can get a better deal if you choose loose produce and get it weighed at the checkout. Not only are you not paying for the packaging, but you are also buying the amount you want and not the amount determined by the packager – which may be too much, or even too little, encouraging you to buy two packs that you don't really need.

Avoid 'Prepared' Fruit and Veg

Seriously, how long does it take to cut up a melon or top and tail beans? You pay heavily for the privilege of having it done for you.

Buy Food in Season

It's cheaper to buy local food in season than food that has been transported halfway across the world – and better for the planet too. Check what's in season at www.eattheseasons.co.uk.

Buy Cheaper Cuts of Meat

Cook them slowly to make them tender. Cheap cuts are just as nutritious and can be just as delicious as expensive ones.

Check out the Delicatessen

You will find loose cheese, cold meats and other deli goods at lower prices than expensively branded goods from the major food manufacturers.

Weigh up the Costs

Supermarkets are legally obliged to state the price per unit of each item, whether it be per kilo or per litre. However, many will use different units, such as using both litres and millilitres for liquids, so you have to do the sums in your head. If you are a dedicated penny-pincher, take a calculator with you to the shops.

Shop Online

You may have to pay a delivery charge, but how much do you usually spend in fuel to get to the out-of-town supermarket? And how much time do you spend when you could usefully be doing something more productive? If you ask for a midweek delivery, you may be able to benefit from a cheaper delivery charge than at the weekend.

Buy Frozen Food

Freezing your own home-grown produce is the cheapest option if you want to maintain a ready supply of fresh vegetables in your home. But if you don't grow your own veg, and you have to rely on a supermarket for your produce, why not buy ready frozen? Studies have shown that frozen food is just as nutritious as fresh food. If you are in a hurry and need only small quantities, buying frozen fruit and vegetables can save money by minimizing waste. Buying frozen special ingredients can also pay dividends – particularly if seeking out the fresh variety from a specialist supplier would involve a separate journey and additional petrol costs.

Buy Bargain Brands

Most big-name supermarkets have a budget or 'value' brand. Often these products are little different from the so-called premium products. Using value products really is a matter of taste – but sometimes this hardly matters. For instance, cheaper tinned tomatoes may have less tomato and more juice in the tin than a premium brand, and you may find a few extra bits of tomato skin left behind from the processing, but if quantity is not an issue and it's no bother to remove the skin residue, then value lines are for you.

✔ **Experiment**: When it comes to flavour, you need to experiment with cheaper brands and non-branded items. A recent blind test performed on a TV consumer show found that more people among those interviewed preferred the taste of non-branded goods than branded goods – although most had said before they took the taste test that they believed the outcome would show that they preferred the branded goods.

✔ **Advice**: *Supermarket Own Brand Guide: Choosing the Best Value Food and Drink,* by Martin Isark (£6.99), is a book that can help you choose which cheaper or non-branded item to buy, as is *The Savvy Shopper* by Rose Prince (£8.99).

Don't Buy Baby Food

Make your own with puréed vegetables and fruits. It's cheaper, you know what's in it and you can cater for your baby's tastes. Ready-prepared jars can be handy for travelling, but are expensive and unnecessary. You can make your own in batches and freeze it.

Don't Buy 'Children's Food'

Food specially marketed for children is a recent invention, designed to part parents from their money. Any item that bears a picture of a cartoon or movie character will cost more because of the licensing fee – so you are essentially paying for the cardboard around the food. Avoid cereals and desserts marketed for children, as they may actually be less healthy than similar 'adult' items, very often containing excessive amounts of sugar. Items marketed as 'lunch box size' are also a rip-off. It may seem 'handy' to drop a little box of raisins into your child's school lunch pack, but how much time does it actually take to grab a handful of raisins out of a larger, cheaper packet? If your child must have a certain item 'because everyone else has them', keep the packaging and refill it yourself.

Use a Supermarket-Comparison Site

If you are not sure where to find the best deals, check out www.mySupermarket.co.uk. This site compares the cost of similar purchases from your local Tesco, Asda, Ocado and Sainsbury's online supermarkets. You can ask it to switch the products you choose for others if there are cheaper brands or alternatives available, and you can also ask the site to find you healthier options. The site also collates the top 100 special offers. Having made your selection from your chosen store, the site will forward your order to the store. You can keep an online shopping list, so you don't have to remember what you need to buy each week. For those who prefer to shop in person rather than online, the site can help you calculate whether you could save money by switching supermarkets.

Time Your Shopping

It's not only market stalls that get rid of their remaining stock at knock-down prices at the end of the day. Supermarkets often clear their shelves of fresh food that is about to exceed it sell-by date in the late afternoon. Supermarket sell-by dates are often cautious, and you should use your common sense about eating it after the designated date. If you store fresh food in your fridge, you should be able to get away with eating it a day or two after the date on the packet – but certainly don't take risks and endanger your health. If there is any indication that the food has gone off – if it has gone a funny colour or smells odd, for example – don't take any chances. Eating bottled or tinned food after its official best-before date should be absolutely fine as long as the containers are not damaged.

Check out the Damaged-Goods Shelf

As well as selling off fresh items cheaply at the end of the day, stores will also probably have a shelf of damaged goods, such as cartons that have been squashed or torn, or food that is about to go out of date. As long as the food inside the packaging is not affected by damage to the carton, there are rich pickings for anyone who wants to save money.

Customer tricks: One canny shopper keeps a couple of old coffee-jar lids at home in her cupboard. Her local supermarket seems to smash the plastic screw-top lids on jars of premium instant coffee on a regular basis. It therefore sells the jars with £1 or so off the usual price. When they go on the shelf, they still have the airtight foil seal intact, but no screw-on lid. The canny shopper snaps up these jars and screws on her own lids as soon as she gets home – and saves herself a fortune on coffee. The same shopper also has a collection of the white nozzles that fit on aerosols to make the spray, the plungers that come with liquid soap and handcream bottles, and an assortment of flip-top screw-on shampoo bottle caps, to replace the broken ones on the other items that she buys from the damaged-goods shelf.

If You Can't Liquidize, Fertilize

Damaged fruit and vegetables can be a good buy for compotes, soups and purées, as you can just cut out the bruised or damaged parts, and use the rest. Bruised and overripe soft fruit can be saved from the compost heap by liquidizing them with a dash of orange juice and making them into delicious smoothies to drink. If fruit and vegetable leftovers and peelings are too far gone to use at all, don't chuck them in the bin. Compost them to boost the yield on your home-grown veg.

Don't Waste Food

Gone are the days when the Sunday joint became cold cuts on Monday, rechauffée on Tuesday, shepherd's pie on Wednesday and curry or pasties on Thursday. How many of us roast a chicken, then throw the bones in the bin instead of boiling them up for stock or soup? Now's the time to get back into good habits.

 Stock: Make stock with chicken carcasses and discarded bits of vegetables. Pick the bones for any meat to use in the contents of a pie.

✔ **Use everything**: Make sure that you use every last scrap in the saucepan rather than filling it up with water to soak before washing. If rice sticks to the pan and you can't scrape it out with a spoon, soak it in a bit of cold water for a few minutes, then drain. You then have another portion of rice that you can heat up in the microwave.

✔ **Cheese**: Grate the dried-up ends of cheese for use in sauces and bakes.

✔ **Wine**: Freeze the dregs of a bottle of wine in an ice-cub etray, and use the tasty ice cubes in soups and casseroles to save opening a bottle for cooking.

✔ **Advice**: If you hate waste, you will love www.lovefoodhatewaste.com, which helps you with recipes, portion planning and reusing leftover food. There are lots of hints, ranging from how to refresh a stale crusty loaf of bread to stopping an avocado turning brown.

Cook Once, Eat Twice

Cook batches of food. If you take advantage of BOGOF offers, buy large-sized packets to save money, or buy in bulk at a discounter (see overleaf). Instead of allowing food you don't need now to go to waste or simply fill up your store cupboards, cook it immediately. If you are making a stew, lasagne, soups or sauces, make double, treble or more than the quantity you need for one meal and freeze the rest (you might not be able to face the same meal three days in a row, so freezing is preferable to leaving it in the fridge). Make sure that you divide the excess into manageable portions to suit the family. You don't want to have to defrost soup for six if there are only two of you. You are not only saving money on ingredients, but you get a home-made ready meal and a night off from cooking at some future date as well.

Buy in Bulk

There are various ways to shop in bulk.

BOGOF

You can make savings at your usual supermarket by buying BOGOF items – buy one, get one free. You can either buy the extra item and keep it in your store cupboard, or go shopping with a friend and share the BOGOF deals. BOGOFs can work out as extremely good value – because they are paid for by the manufacturer. When margins are tight, supermarkets want reduced prices, but the manufacturers, who are keen to protect their profits, will balk at this. However, they may be able to strike a deal. If the supermarket can deliver a 20% increase in sales, the manufacturer may be persuaded to cut the item price because he can gain market share and keep his factory workers busy. This is good news for you – but only if you or your friend can use the second item.

Shopping for One

If shopping just for yourself, buy large quantities of perishable items only if you are prepared to cook them immediately or share the bulk (see below).

Sharing

If you belong to a community or club, you may be able to make bulk purchases and share the cost between you. If you live alone, consider sharing a shopping trip with a friend and splitting special offers and large packets. If you travel together to the supermarket, you will save on petrol at the same time, if you are travelling by car.

Look out for Small Packs on Special Offer

While buying larger quantities and larger pack sizes usually works out cheaper, supermarkets often discount small-sized packets in a special offer. Don't be caught out buying a large packet when two smaller ones could have been cheaper. For instance, at the time of writing Asda is offering a 500g jar of Marmite yeast extract spread for £4.59, but 250g jars cost £2. So buying two smaller jars would be cheaper – and probably more convenient – than buying the large size.

Go Wholesale

If you want to shop in bulk seriously, you need to go to a wholesaler – the sort that supplies local shops and caterers. Ones with national coverage include Makro (www.makro.co.uk) and Costco (www.costco.co.uk). You need to have your own business or be self-employed to use a wholesaler, and be able to provide evidence (details of what you need as evidence are on the companies' websites). But if you are able to do this, or you can join forces with someone who can do this, you can then make big savings.

Don't Fall for the Supermarket Tricks

Supermarkets are in business to part you from your money. They use tricks including music, special lighting and attractive displays to point you towards certain purchases. Your job as a credit-crunch shopper is to get what you need and just what you need, without buying any excess to requirements or paying more for the items that you do need to buy. Follow the psychological supermarket code.

Don't Go At All!

Don't go to the supermarket if all you need is a pint of milk. You are bound to come out with more than you intended. If you walk to the corner shop for the milk, you may save petrol too.

Eat Before You Shop

Research has shown that people who shop when they are hungry spend more and buy more than they need. Shop on a full stomach.

Plan Future Meals Before You Shop

Make out a meal plan for the week. That way you get the right combination of ingredients and don't find yourself left with a bag of vegetables or a pack of minced beef and no forthcoming meal to use it for. Food in the bin is money down the drain and wasteful.

Compile a Shopping List

It sounds obvious, but a shopping list is not only to remind you to buy the things you need – and is clearly a good idea if you have planned your meals as suggested above – but it should also help you to avoid buying the things you don't need, which is a major contributor to wasting your hard-earned cash.

Special Offers

Be wary of them! Do you know the price that you usually pay before you plump for a BOGOF (buy one, get one free)? If you end up paying more than the price for one item, and the second item ends up in the bin, you have not saved money. Equally, if the offer tempts you to buy a branded item that you would not usually buy, you could end up paying more than sticking to your usual purchase.

Avoid Glittering Displays

Manufacturers pay a premium for certain display points in supermarkets. You will find the latest 'new' products in bright packages at eye level, where you can spot them easily. If you need a certain product, whether it be yoghurt or furniture polish, look on the lower shelves to see if you can find an equivalent product – perhaps the supermarket's own brand – at a lower price. It is the contents not the packaging that is important.

Don't Be Tempted by Confectionery and Other Items near the Checkout

Supermarkets have come under fire for putting sweets at the level where children in pushchairs can see them, thereby subjecting their parents to pester power. Supermarkets have hit back by putting other knicknacks around the checkout. While it may be convenient for some shoppers, it is temptation to others. If you buy something at the checkout, be sure it is an item you would have bought anyway if you had remembered it earlier, and is not a more expensive brand.

'Free' Food

Whether by putting in a little effort in the garden or by learning how to spot the edible plants that surround us in nature, there are many ways you can source food that is either free or almost so, save for the cost of some seeds.

Grow Your Own Veg

This is probably not a route for anyone but the gardening enthusiast, but you will save pounds and gain great satisfaction from growing your own fruit and vegetables. NS&I, which sponsors the Royal Horticultural Society's Grow Your Own Veg campaign, estimates that, if you make your own lunch every day from vegetables you have grown yourself, instead of paying a daily visit to the sandwich shop, you could save nearly £1,000 a year, and more than £35,000 during your working lifetime.

- **Allotments**: If you don't have a garden, contact your local council to find out how to apply for an allotment. Allotments are usually available at a very reasonable rent, and produce additional benefits, including companionship and healthy exercise in an outdoor environment.

- **Window box**: If gardening is not for you, then even growing your own herbs in a window box will save you money compared with paying supermarket prices.

 Sharing: If you live in an upstairs flat which overlooks an unkempt garden because the people downstairs don't take care of it, ask them if you can cultivate the garden for them in exchange for a share of the produce.

Drink Tap Water

Tests have proved that there's no real difference between tap water and bottled water when it comes to your wellbeing. Yet as a nation we spent £1.68bn on 2.275 billion litres of bottled water in 2006. Some bottled water is tap water anyway, with added carbonation. Fancy mineral waters are an unnecessary, expensive luxury for the credit-crunch saver. So drink tap water, which is just as good for you and more environmentally friendly because there is no bottle to transport or dispose of.

Send Away for Free Food

Use a website such as www.foodfreebies.co.uk or www.sendmediscounts.co.uk to track down introductory offers, free samples and discounted food.

Scavenge for Free Food

'Freegans', also known as 'dumpster divers', 'bin divers' or 'skippers', are consumer activists who, among other anti-waste activities, raid supermarket rubbish bins after the store has closed to find discarded food that is still edible. Unfortunately this cannot be recommended, as the practice is generally judged to be illegal in the UK and is technically theft, particularly where the bins are situated on private land, and where opening a covered bin can be deemed to be breaking and entering. You can, however, still scavenge for plenty of food that is free perfectly legally.

Hunt for Free Food in Nature

A more legal, fun and natural way to source free food is to head into the country or any public natural space and seek out edible plants and fungi.

 Books: Richard Mabey's book *Food for Free*, which was first published in 1972, gives details of more than 300 types of food that can be gathered in the wild in Britain, with details on how to pick, when to pick and regulations on picking. Other 'free food' books include Hugh Fearnley Whittingstall's *A Cook on the Wild Side*, or, for the more adventurous, read Ray Mears' *Wild Food* to find out how to survive in the wild on nature's bounty, or the similarly named *Wild Food* by Roger Phillips. Buy them on Amazon or via another online book discounter to save money – or, better still, pick them up second-hand. *The Essential Nettle, Dandelion, Chickweed & Thistle Cookbook* by Johnny Jumbalaya is currently out of print, but you can get lots of his recipes for wild food on www.countrylovers.co.uk.

Courses: Marcus Harrison runs the Wild Food School at Lostwithiel in Cornwall (telephone 01208 873 788 or email wildfoodie@yahoo.co.uk).

 Caution: Do watch out for poisonous plants, and eat wild mushrooms only if you are sure you have identified them correctly. Don't eat anything that you are not sure about if you are pregnant, breastfeeding or have any other condition, and don't give such food to children.

Make Your Own Wine and Beer

Rustic types can make elderberry or parsnip wine, or you can buy kits with the juices you need. Wine-and-beer-making kits are available from high-street chemist shops such as Boots, many health food shops and specialist suppliers. Details from www.homewinemaking.co.uk. If you are a beer drinker, you can save more than £2 a pint by brewing your own. Get more information from www.homebeermaking.co.uk, www.Art-of-Brewing.co.uk and www.jimsbeerkit.co.uk.

Where to Shop

Don't automatically assume your local supermarket will have the best deals – try to shop around and resist the allure of convenience.

Shop in Markets

It is only when you visit a market that you realize how much you are paying in supermarkets for cellophane-wrapped produce. For the best bargains, shop towards the end of the day when stallholders are trying to get rid of the last of their stock. You will get great bunches of bananas for less than £1 and bags of apples and tomatoes for 50p. If you buy potatoes that still have soil on them, keep them in the dark, preferably in brown paper or sacking, and they will keep for ages compared with the ready-washed spuds that you get in plastic bags in the supermarkets, which soon go mushy.

Use Budget Shops

As detailed in the Shopping section (pages 68–71), the budget supermarkets have come a long way from when they were the shop of choice for only very-low-income families. They are now giving the big-brand supermarkets a serious run for their money. Lidl was recently named the best value-for-money retailer by the consumer organization Which?. The stores are less than elegant – to save staff time, and you money, things are usually sold out of the box – and you need to pay for carrier bags. Although they accept debit cards, you can't pay by credit card. But the savings on offer make up for any inconvenience.

A calculator on the home page of the Aldi website claims that a 30-year-old female shopper spending an average of £130 a week in a mainstream supermarket could save £86,697 during the course of her lifetime if she switched her custom to Aldi. True, she would have only 1,100 different lines to choose from, rather than as many as 30,000 products available in a typical supermarket, and familiar branded goods would be few and far between, if not nonexistent, but Aldi says it guarantees that filling your trolley in its aisles will cost you 20 per cent less than if you went to one of the big-name supermarkets. In Which?'s research of 15 shopping basket items, Aldi came out cheapest on five items and Lidl cheapest on three. Tesco, which has cut prices to try to match the popularity of the low-cost stores, came out cheapest on only two – milk chocolate digestive biscuits and mature Cheddar.

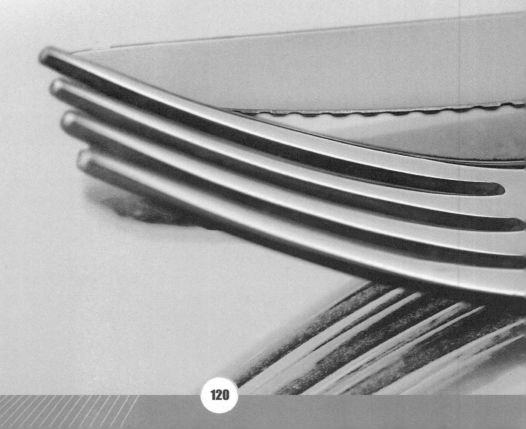

Experiment: When shopping in these budget stores, you will need to experiment a bit to see what suits your tastes, but you will find fruit and vegetables of remarkably good quality, and while cooked meats and dairy products may have unfamiliar branding they are generally just as good as – and sometimes better than – more expensive items in other supermarkets.

Recipe help: You can find recipes for using mostly Lidl ingredients at www.lidl-recipes.co.uk. Aldi has a similar recipe site at www.aldirecipesonline.com.

Upmarket: Goods are not just downmarket items either. You can find Champagne, exotic seafood and extra virgin olive oil at both Lidl and Aldi. *Woman* magazine said of Lidl Bisinger Premium Cuvée: 'If you like bubbly dry, you'll love this. Tangy and sharp, and the bottle shape hides the budget background. A Champagne to fool your guests.'

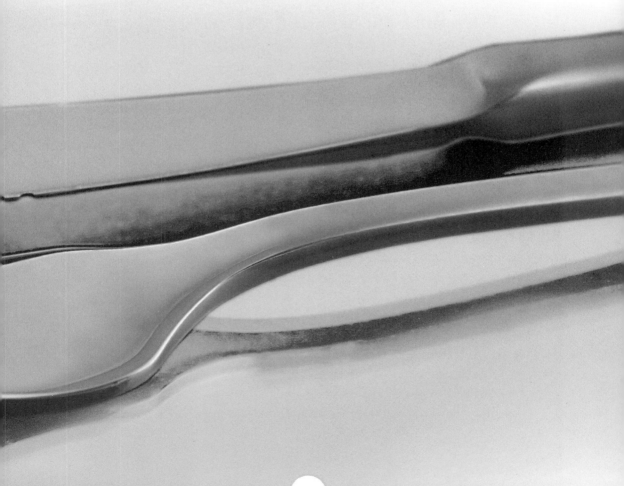

Best buys: Look out especially for the supermarkets' best buys. Lidl jaffa cakes were given a score of 4.5 out of 5 in a tasting test conducted by the *Bournemouth Daily Echo*. The paper concluded: 'Not much between these and the M&S ones, but these take the biscuit on price.'

Keep down the Cost of Eating Out

Just because you're tightening the purse strings, doesn't mean you have to avoid eating out entirely. Just bear in mind some useful points.

Look out for Set Menus at Restaurants

You may get special offers on lunch, pre-theatre or even some dinner menus. The *Good Food Guide* gives suggestions for good-value set menus. Also, use a website such as www.toptable.co.uk to find good deals in your area. In addition, www.lastminute.com often gives details of restaurants that offer special deals in combination with a special offer of tickets for a show.

Use Vouchers

Two-for-one vouchers and 'Lunch for a Fiver' or 'Lunch for £10' offers appear regularly in national newspapers. Look out for them in the papers or the voucher websites.

 Examples: Restaurants chains that offer discounts from time to time include Pizza Express, Strada, Giraffe, Café Rouge, La Tasca, Loch Fyne and Burger King. Yo! Sushi offers 25 per cent off for students.

 Find more: You can get more information on www.stuff4nowt.co.uk/vouchers.html and www.moneysavingexpert.com in the Discount Code & Voucher Finder forum.

Drink Water

See page 115 above on avoiding bottled water. Restaurants make most of their profits on drinks, especially house wine, which has an average of a 300-per-cent mark-up. If you really want to save money, ask for a glass of tap water with your meal.

Watch out for Extra Service Charges

While this is no place to argue whether restaurants should include service charges in their bill, you should be sure that you don't add a second one on top when they do – particularly when paying by credit card. When a service charge is included, you should not leave a tip for the wait staff as well.

Fast Food

If you just want a sandwich and a coffee, take it away and consume it on a park bench to save money. If you eat inside a coffee shop or sandwich bar, VAT will be added to your bill, increasing what you pay by 17.5 per cent.

Household & Utilities

Cleaning

It is important to keep our homes and clothes clean, but it's not necessary to use the expensive cleaning products which the big multinational companies are constantly trying to flog us. For starters, you could use unbranded products from cheap supermarkets. Most are just as effective as the big-name brands. Indeed, many are exactly the same, just without the fancy expensive packaging. But you could also cut cleaning costs by using alternative products – often things you already have lying around the home.

Use Cheaper Cleaning Products

Look at the supermarket shelves these days. They're crammed with cleaning products for specific purposes. Toilet cleaners, bathroom cleaners, kitchen worktop cleaners, floor cleaners and even kitchen-sink cleaners. There are special sprays and wipes for any kind of cleaning you can think of – but they are all largely designed to encourage us to part with more cash than we need to. Our grandparents and parents never had such a choice, and frankly never needed it.

Buy Generic

Rather than specific cleaners for all parts of the house, buy generic cleaners. They'll do the job just as well and be much cheaper. And you won't end up with a kitchen or bathroom cupboard full of different coloured bottles and aromas!

Buy Own Brand

Even better is buying unbranded cleaners from budget supermarkets. They really will do the job just as well.

Use Alternative Cleaning Products

You could even make your own cleaning fluids to save even more money. What did people used to use? Cheap items such as vinegar, baking soda, bleach, club soda and ammonia. Look around your home – you probably already have several useful things that can be adapted for cleaning purposes. Ask parents or grandparents for more tips like the ones below – they may have lots of old-style cleaning methods that can help to save you pounds.

Lemon Juice

Garlic can be a problem when it stains a chopping board and makes everything else smell. But a cheap solution is a simple lemon. Cut it in half and run it across the board – the garlicky smell will very quickly disappear. A cheap bottle of lemon juice is also good for cleaning stubborn spots on copper and brass, and saves the expense of buying branded cleaners.

Tea Tree on Trainers

Another nasty odour to contend with is whiffy trainers. There are some decent shoe deodorants you can buy which control the smell. But there's no need to spend the cash. Instead, simply get a small bottle of tea tree oil and sprinkle a few drops inside the offending footwear. Sorted!

White Vinegar

White vinegar is perfect for cleaning windows and glass. And it costs considerably less than supermarket-bought glass cleaner. It is also a cheap and effective alternative to dishwasher water-softening agents. There really is no need to pay out pounds for these when running your washer empty with a cupful of vinegar will do the trick. It will keep the dishwasher clean, as well as keep the limescale to a minimum. The same goes for washing machines.

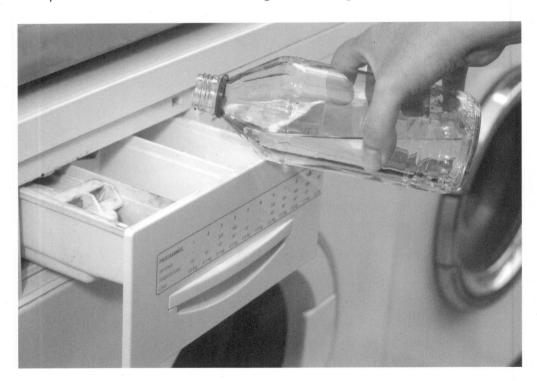

Alternative Cloths

Don't buy expensive cloths to clean glass – use an old screwed-up sheet of newspaper. You'll be surprised at how gleaming glass and mirrors come up. Talking of cloths, don't be tempted to buy expensive dusters and cleaning cloths. Instead, check in your wardrobe for those old T-shirts, sweatshirts and cotton tops that you'll never wear again. Cut them up and use them instead. They do the job very well.

Antibacterial Cleaning

Look at the expensive antibacterial sprays that lots of families use these days. They're very convenient – but they are expensive. A bowl of hot soapy washing-up liquid with a splash of bleach does the job perfectly well – and at much less than half the cost.

Removing Limescale

And what about the bottles of limescale remover that a lot of people have? Save money by using a pumice stone instead. It's not only cheaper, but better for your home as it won't scratch enamel. Pumice is harder than limescale so will remove it, but softer than the surface you are using it on.

Cleaning Pans

You should also keep a bottle or can of cola to hand to use to clean burnt pans. Simply pour the fizzy pop into the pan and bring it to the boil, then leave it to stand for a few minutes. Wipe around afterwards, and the burnt stuff should simply wipe away. Or, when scrubbing pots, don't splash out on scouring pads. Instead use the net bags which a lot of fruit and vegetables come in. As scourers, they're pretty effective.

Use Traditional Stain Removers

Try the following traditional tricks:

 Blood: A little spot of blood on clothes? The cheapest cleaner of all is your own spit. A little bit of saliva on the spot should clean it quite efficiently.

White shirts: If you have a stained white shirt, go to the fridge and get out the milk. Yes, milk is reasonably effective at combating stains on white shirts. The same milk should be brought out to remove any spots of ink on your sofa. Although, if you have no milk to hand, hairspray could do the trick.

Grease on cotton: For a greasy spot on a cotton dress, turn to washing-up liquid. Get it a little foamy on a cloth, then dab at the spot. After a minute or two of your dabbing, you should be able to rinse out the now spot-free dress with cold water.

Red wine: If you spill red wine on clothing or carpets, reach for the white wine or salt. Pour some white straight on top of the red, and the stain should simply vanish. Afterwards, wipe away the wine with a wet cloth. If you pour table salt on the stain, it will absorb the wine. Leave it to dry, then either vacuum the salt up – if it's a carpet – or brush away the salt, then wash the clothing.

Decorating

Homes need to be decorated every so often, and there are always odd bits of repair work that need to be done. If you've been used to simply calling someone up to do these types of jobs, it's time to take care of them yourself and save a packet.

Why Redecorate and How?

It is important to maintain your home to a decent standard. Let things drift, and small problems will get worse and pretty soon your smart home could begin to look a bit dilapidated. That could cost you thousands when it comes to selling as no one will pay the top price for a home that looks a bit of a shambles. But of more pressing concern is the fact that, if you don't keep your home up to scratch regularly, what could have been a series of small jobs could end up being major work – which could run into thousands of pounds. Spending a little time giving your home some tender, loving care will pay you in the long term through it increasing in value, but also reduce the chance of problems developing into a renovation project, with its own attendant problems and huge expense.

Be Realistic about Do-It-Yourself

You can cut the cost of redecorating by doing it yourself. It's a simple solution, but its practicality could depend on how useful you are with a paintbrush. You need to be completely honest with yourself before tackling any decorating or DIY job. Can you honestly do it? Or could your efforts make things worse and lead to the expense of getting someone else in to put things right?

Be Prepared

The secret is to prepare well and take things at a steady pace. If you're doing it yourself, you can set your own deadlines, so give yourself as long as you need, which is likely to be longer than you expect! Think the job through, rather than rushing in. Preparation is key to avoiding costly mistakes and wasting your time and money.

Redecorating on the Cheap

The quickest way to spruce up your home is to box up all your clutter and give the place a good scrub. Pay attention to detail, and attack the limescale marks in sinks and toilets, and greasy cooker hobs and ovens.

Quality

If the walls need a new coat of paint, make sure to buy the best paint and brushes you can afford. It's a false economy to buy cheap paint and brushes. Cheap, thin paints need more coats and therefore often work out more expensive than dearer paints. Cheap brushes moult on walls – often meaning you need to repaint almost at once. Also, they won't last longer than one application.

Brush Care

Brush care is important if you want to avoid having to splash out on lots of replacement brushes. After using a brush, clean it thoroughly in water, then wrap the brush head in a piece of newspaper. Do this, and the brush will retain its shape and will be easier to use the second, third and fourth times around, leaving you no need to buy a replacement.

Masking Tape

Here's a tip – invest in a roll of masking tape. It's essential wherever you need to protect a surface while working on another – for instance, if you are painting the skirting board and need to protect the carpet below or wallpaper above. Preparation is important, and you should clean all surfaces with sugar soap first. You may even need to get some sandpaper to smooth down some surfaces before you clean them with sugar soap. Don't be tempted to leave out this part and go straight on to slapping on the paint. The finish will be dreadful and may even look worse than before, and you will have to spend more time and money doing it again.

Keep Things Simple

For the best effect, avoid bright colours and splashes of individualism. Just keep things neutral. Use only white emulsion for ceilings, and white gloss for woodwork such as skirting boards and windows.

Painting Dark Surfaces

If you're covering dark walls, it's actually cheaper to do the first coat with white emulsion, before painting over a second coat using the more expensive, coloured paint. If you need to retouch a small area, you may be able to use leftover paint, rather than spending more money on a new tin. But strain the old paint through the leg of a pair of tights to remove all the lumps first, otherwise the lumps will only end up on the wall.

Gardening

Gardening can be a great deal of fun – but it can be expensive. You can turn things around by making the garden work for you producing food and herbs. You'll get lots of pleasure out of saving money this way.

Growing Your Own

Food bills seems to rise every week. But you can save a lot by growing your own vegetables. Obviously the amount you can grow will be limited by the space you have available. But even the smallest city gardens or window sills have room for a few herbs.

Organic

If you can grow your own, there are other benefits to be had in addition to the cash you'll save. For starters, you'll be growing chemical-free produce, which should make for tasty food.

Children's Health

Growing your own veg is also great in helping children try different greens. Involve them in the process, and they will hardly be able to wait to try what comes out of the ground.

Marrows and Beans

Marrows and courgettes are plants that the children will like to grow. They need very little looking after except plenty of watering and harvesting – and they look fantastic. Runner beans are another easy option and just keep on coming, producing some spectacular growth in a relatively short space of time.

Potatoes

Potatoes can be grown from old peelings, as long as they have the 'eyes' in. Save them in a dark bag and, when you have enough, dig a thin trench in the garden and sprinkle the peelings in. It won't be long before little new potatoes appear.

Herbs

Herbs can be grown in pots, then picked when needed. Mint, parsley and chives are very easy to grow and add taste to lots of different recipes. If you have an old wheelbarrow, drill holes in it for drainage and fill it with soil – it then becomes an interesting and perfect herb garden.

Cheap Gardening

Ant Killer

Don't buy expensive ant killer. Use talcum powder instead – it has exactly the same effect.

Hanging Baskets

If you're making hanging baskets, don't waste cash on basket liners. Instead line the baskets with an old knitted sweater.

Sprayers

Don't buy these. Simple thoroughly wash any domestic cleaning sprayers and use them instead.

Compost

Start a compost heap to provide you with rich material to feed your garden with. It needn't cost you a penny. Use old wood to make the bin and use old carpet for the floor – it'll keep in the heat generated by the rotting material. Make layers of grass cuttings, weeds and vegetable waste from the kitchen. Keep topping it up, and before long you'll have fresh, free well-rotted compost for your garden.

Energy

Gas and electricity bills are rocketing. The average annual energy bill is approaching near £1,500 towards the end of 2008 as domestic fuel prices have climbed around a third over the year. But a quick bit of shopping around and switching supplier could save you hundreds. You could also save energy and money by making your home more fuel-efficient and cutting back on waste.

Switch to Save

It looks like we may well be set for a world where gas and electricity prices continue to climb. That means you have to check your prices and compare them with others, and if appropriate switch suppliers. If you haven't switched supplier for years, you will almost certainly discover that there's a better deal for you – often saving hundreds of pounds a year. If you have switched supplier – even if it was fairly recently – it's still well worth shopping around. New deals come and go all the time, and you are still likely to discover that you can save money by switching.

Direct Debit Savings

You can get extra discounts, for instance, if you pay by direct debit or manage your account online. According to recent figures, an average dual-fuel user – who has both gas and electricity – could save around £162 by choosing an online direct debit tariff. And that's just the average saving – you could be looking at even bigger reductions.

Price-Comparison Websites

There is a range of online comparison sites where you can put in your postcode and your

average energy usage, and they will come up with a range of different options for you. Try sites such as www.uswitch.com or www.moneysupermarket.com for a range of different options that could help you to switch gas and electricity providers to get a better deal.

Make Your Home More Efficient

The Energy Saving Trust says the average household could save up to £250 a year on energy bills by making their home more energy-efficient.

Turn down the Thermostat

Turn down your thermostat by 1°C, for example. It will cut your heating bills by 10 per cent, and save you at least £40 a year. If you don't tell anyone you've done so, it's unlikely they will notice. But you will notice the extra cash!

Roof, Wall and Floor Insulation

Insulating your home is one of the most effective ways of improving the energy efficiency of it. For example, insulating a loft can save around £155 a year by reducing heat loss. For best protection, ensure your loft has 25 cm (10 in) of insulation. Around a third of all the heat lost in an uninsulated home is actually lost through the walls. You can reduce the heat loss – and save money – by putting in cavity wall insulation. It could save you around £120 a year on

your fuel bills. Look down too. Lots of heat escapes through gaps around skirting boards and floors. But they are simple to fix yourself with a tube of sealant bought from most DIY stores. You could save around £40 a year by insulating your floors.

Pipe Insulation

You should also lag your hot-water cylinder and pipes, including those in your loft. Both tank and pipe insulation keep your water hotter for longer by reducing the amount of heat that escapes.

Draught-proofing

Similar in effect to insulation, draught-proofing helps to seal gaps around windows and doors. In a typical home 20 per cent of all heat loss is through poor ventilation and draughts. If everyone in the UK adopted a few simple draught-proofing measures in their homes, such as fitting brushes to letterboxes, together we'd save around £160m per year, according to the Energy Saving Trust!

Double Glazing

It may have a bad reputation because of pushy salespeople turning up on your doorstep, but double glazing can actually improve the energy efficiency of your home. It works by trapping air between two panes of glass, creating an insulating barrier that reduces heat loss, noise and condensation. In the process, double glazing cuts heat lost through windows by half – which could save around £110 a year on your heating bills. If you live in a terraced house, you could even turn off your heat and use the warmth from your neighbours' houses.

Curtains

Remember to draw the curtains at dusk every day. Doing so reduces heat loss by 40 per cent for single-glazed windows and 30 per cent for double-glazed windows. And, although it may seem obvious, remember to check windows and not leave them open when the heating is on.

Electricity Waste

Think about the amount of electricity you use. You can cut bills by avoiding leaving appliances on stand-by. Turn off all your electronic equipment – especially computers, TVs, radios and DVDs that you usually leave on standby. Even when they're not on, they're draining the juice and costing you money. Also, boil only enough water for your needs when making a cup of tea or coffee. Just fill a mug with water before putting it into the kettle for each cup you're making.

Ironing

You can save more energy – and the misery of ironing – by stretching clothes out and hanging them straight on the line or clothes rack when you take them out of the washing machine. In most cases you won't need to iron them once thy are dry.

Lights

Turn off lights, too, when you're leaving the room. You're wasting electricity if you leave them on when you're not there. And switching to energy-saving light bulbs in your home could save you hundreds of pounds. Just one can save £100 over the lifetime of the bulb – and they last up to 12 times longer than ordinary light bulbs.

Get Cash to Make Home Improvements

You can get cash to help you make energy-saving improvements to your home. The government, energy suppliers and local authorities all provide grants to help you implement energy-saving measures in your home. If you're on benefits, for instance, you may be able to claim up to £2,700 to improve your heating and energy efficiency under the Warm Front scheme. If you have a low income, your energy supplier may help to improve the energy efficiency of your home free of charge. Contact your local Energy Efficiency Advice Centre or the Home Heat Helpline on 0800 33 66 99.

Do You Use Oil to Heat Your Home?

Lots of people in rural areas do. If you're one of them, try www.boilerjuice.co.uk. It's an internet oil company that provides heating oil

to homes across the country at lower prices. It does so by comparing fuel prices and seeking out discount deals. If you buy direct from a local supplier, it pays to pit one local firm against another, and bargain for the best price you can get. If you want to save money on home oil, you'll have to learn to haggle!

Buy Boiler Cover

Spending money to save money? It may sound an odd concept, but when it comes to your boiler it could make sense. What happens if your boiler breaks down? It's a costly business getting it repaired – even if you can find a plumber you trust to do the work. Many people are forced to use the Yellow Pages and, while it's possible you might get lucky and find someone honest who can do a good job for a fair price, there are many cowboys out there who simply want to rip you off. A typical trick is to say that you need a new boiler – which could cost £1,500 or more. In reality, you may just need a new part or some tweaks to the system to get it working properly again.

In 2007, British Gas was called out more than 60,000 times a week for emergency boiler repairs during the winter – at a wallet-stretching average cost of £185. In fact costs of repairs to a boiler tops £470. But you can get a simple insurance policy for around £10 a month which covers the cost of call-outs and repairs – and guarantees a honest trades person. Most energy suppliers have a scheme which could save you a packet in the long term, as well as giving you peace of mind that your boiler will be repaired or replaced if it breaks. But it's well worth shopping around among independent companies that offer similar policies and often at much cheaper prices than the large energy suppliers.

Where to Go for More Help

For advice on making your home more efficient, head online to:

✅ **Energy Saving Trust**: Its website, www.energysavingtrust.org.uk, is packed with ways to help you save energy and money in the home. You can also get a free home energy check by calling 0800 512 012. Just answer some simple questions about your home, and you'll receive a free, impartial report telling you how you can save up to £300 a year on your household energy bills.

✅ **Warm Front**: To find out about government grants and financial help with heating, go to www.warmfront.co.uk or ring 0800 316 6007.

Water

Each of us currently uses about 150 litres of water every day! If that sounds a lot, think about the amount of water we waste down the plughole as we brush our teeth or wash our face – or the gallons being flushed away each time we use the toilet. The amount of water we use has been rising by 1 per cent a year since 1930, according to the Energy Saving Trust – but just a few small changes in your home can cut down on waste and, if you install a meter, slash water bills.

Installing a Meter

Consider installing a water meter; it could really help cut down on your bills. As a rule of thumb, anyone with a large house with only a few occupants would be better off with a meter. The water regulator Ofwat advises that single occupiers are most likely to benefit from having a water meter, while large families may be worse off. You can find out either by asking your water supplier to calculate how a meter would affect your charges or checking for yourself with the Consumer Council for Water's online calculator, which you will find at www.ccwater.or.uk. The council says a single person living in a property with an average rateable value could save around £100 a year by having a meter installed.

Take a Shower

Showers use a lot less water than baths and can really help cut down on your water usage over time. A bath can use more than 100 litres of water, while a shower uses only a third of that amount. However, be wary of happily showering away thinking you're saving cash. If you have a power shower and stay under it for more than five minutes, you'll use more water than a

bath. But you can also save water at the same time by taking a large plastic storage box with you into the shower. The water that collects in the box can be reused to top up the toilet cistern or to water your garden or household plants.

Repairs

You would be surprised how a few basic repairs can cut down water wastage. Check all the taps in your home. Replacing washers could solve the problem of dripping taps – which produce a steady stream of wastage over time. In fact a dripping tap can waste as much as 5,500 litres of water a year, according to the Energy Saving Trust – which is enough to fill a paddling pool every week for the whole summer. Repairing just one dripping tap could save you more than £18 a year if you're on a meter.

Waste Less

If you do install the meter, you can really help to bring down the cost of water by cutting back on your usage. That doesn't mean using less water in practical terms – just wasting less.

- **Running taps**: If you turn off the tap while you're brushing your teeth, for instance, you could save wasting six litres of water a minute.

- **Cistern water**: Put a hippo, save-a-flush or other water displacement device into the cistern. Contact your water company – they should provide the device for free.

- **Dishwashers**: If you have a dishwasher, make sure you always fill it up before running it through a washing cycle. The same is true with washing machines. A full load uses less water than two half-loads.

- **Water-efficient choices**: And when it comes to buying new machines – dishwashers or washing machines – choose a machine based on its water efficiency for future savings. Cut down on water waste by just 10 per cent, and you'll save around £25 a year, according to the Consumer Council for Water.

Where to Go for More Help

At www.waterwise.org.uk you'll find lots more tips on saving water and water efficiency. Or go to www.savewatersavemoney.co.uk for advice and water-saving products for your kitchen and bathroom.

Phone and Broadband

It seems everyone has a mobile and is online these days, but keeping in constant touch can be expensive. That means it's essential to find out what the best deals are and switch to save. The key is to work out how and when you need to use your phone. Ideally you'd use it only to take calls, but that's not a very practical solution to cutting the costs.

Do You Really Need a Phone?

It's a serious question. Whether you have a pay-as-you go or annual contract on a mobile, or use only your phone at home, it's an expensive business. If you could cut the phone altogether, you'd obviously save a packet.

Questions to Ask

For many, having no phone may not be a solution – in which case the only way to cut the costs of using a phone is to pay for only what you need. That means examining your use. Are you constantly texting, for instance? Or do you prefer to ring your friends and have long chats with them? Will you want to use your mobile phone abroad? Or make lots of international calls from your home phone? Answering these questions will help you to track down a deal better suited to the way you really use your phone. You may find that you would be better off with a pay-as-you-go phone, for instance. Or you could even get a free SIM card to put in an old mobile phone to save even more cash.

Cutting Phone and Broadband Costs

Once you have decided what services you need, there are ways to keep costs to a minimum.

Just Use the Mobile

Let's face it, the cost of using a mobile has really come down as competition has gone up. In fact you could save a tenner a month at a stroke by doing away with your home phone line and just using your mobile. It would mean paying no more line rental, which could save you up to £120 a year.

Get a 'Bundle'

On the other hand, if you really want to keep your home phone line – and you'll need to if you want to have broadband at home – then you should be looking at 'bundled' packages. These are where home phone companies and cable firms, as well as mobile operators, offer cheaper fixed costs if you take two or three of their services. So you could save by linking your mobile to your home phone and broadband. Link your satellite or cable TV deal into the same package, and you could save even more. Anyone using all four services to an average extent could save up to £200 a year by bundling.

It's also worth looking at your TV package. If you're paying out for satellite or cable, why not switch to Freeview or Freesat? You will have no more monthly payments, but still be able to choose from tens of different channels. Go to the comparison sites at www.simplifydigital.co.uk or www.broadbandsuppliers.co.uk to compare costs.

Get a 'Dongle'

Installing broadband at home can be an expensive business, with set-up and installation costs to pay for and costly helplines you have to call if you get into difficulties. But you could save money buy signing up for mobile broadband and a 'dongle'. With a simple dongle – a USB device that plugs into your laptop – you can connect to your phone network anywhere.

Cheap: With prices starting from a tenner a month, choosing this option could also work out cheaper than installing a broadband link at home. Combine it with a mobile phone for on-the-move connectivity, and you can do away altogether with your home phone line rental to save £10 a month.

Flexible: If you move around a lot – if you're a student, for instance – it makes more financial sense to invest in a dongle rather than having to pay set-up costs for a broadband service every time you move.

Good alternative: If you live in an area where conventional broadband is still not available, using a dongle could be a cheaper solution that paying for an old-fashioned slow dial-up service.

Don't Call Expensive Numbers

It's a sad fact of modern life that the companies which you do business with use whatever means they can to squeeze extra cash out of you. So if you need to call them to discuss your service, or your bank account, they make you call expensive premium numbers. It's simply a rip-off, and there's no need for them to make you pay these extra charges, apart from inflating their already massive profits. You can beat them at their own game by going online to www.saynoto0870.com. A lot of companies use 0870 numbers, which can cost about 15p a minute. At this website you simply type in the name of the company you want to call, and you get a list of its cheaper geographical numbers – and there are even some free 0800 numbers. You'll not only save cash, but get one back at the big rip-off firms as well!

Where Next?

Go online to compare costs of home phones, mobiles and broadband:

- **www.fone-deals.co.uk**
- **www.cheapest-utility-suppliers.co.uk**
- **www.moneysupermarket.com**
- **www.simplifydigital.co.uk**
- **www.broadbandsuppliers.co.uk**

Transport

Travel for Free

The credit-crunch driver has a number of choices. He or she can abandon the car altogether and walk or use alternative, cheaper transport; trade down to a more modest model; or keep the same car and adopt better techniques, such as changing driving style to reduce fuel consumption, and opening the window instead of reaching for the air-con switch. Let's start with the most drastic option.

Under Your Own Steam

This has to be the ultimate way of saving money on travel, while getting health benefits into the bargain.

Walking

You don't just save money on the car and associated expenses, such as parking and congestion charges: walking brings all sorts of other benefits, such as improving your health, which can have a knock-on effect on life insurance premiums. Walking, amazingly, can sometimes be quicker and more convenient, when you take into account the time spent looking for a parking place and the distance you may need to park from your destination.

Cycle to Work

Ask your employers if they offer cycle leasing under the Cycle to Work Scheme. The scheme, which is a 'salary sacrifice' arrangement, allows employees to lease a bicycle from their employer or the employer's agent for a typical period of 12 or 18 months, after which they may buy the bicycle outright for a nominal price. The only condition of using the scheme for bike purchase is that the bicycle being leased must be used for travel to and from work.

 Tax savings: The employee pays for this through a reduction in salary – the so-called 'salary sacrifice' – eventually paying the full price of the cycle over the lease period. The employee saves on income tax and National Insurance contributions because their salary is reduced by the 'sacrifice'. The employer also saves on National Insurance contributions.

 What's covered: The scheme covers bicycles and safety equipment, including helmets, bells, horns, lights, reflectors, mirrors, mudguards, racks, panniers, straps, clips, locks, chains, pumps, puncture kits, tools and reflective clothing, usually up to a maximum total value of £1,000. While there is actually no legal maximum limit on the value of the equipment leased, the employer would need a Consumer Credit Licence for items of a value greater than £1,000. Up to £1,000 firms are covered by an employers' group licence, issued by the Office of Fair Trading for the purpose of implementing the scheme.

Buses for Young and Old

For longer journeys walking and cycling may be impractical, and you will be forced to use public transport. People of certain ages can qualify for free travel:

Over 60s/65s

England: Since 1 April 2008 everyone who is resident in England and who is more than 60 years of age or disabled has been entitled to a free annual bus pass, giving free off-peak bus travel anywhere in England. If you qualify for a pass, you should apply for one even if you never travel by bus in off-peak hours, or indeed at all, because some local authorities offer extra benefits, such as free travel during peak times or reduced price rail travel. But these will apply only for travel in the local area, and not everywhere in England. Check with your local authority to find out whether you can get extra services.

Wales: In Wales, if you're over 60 you're entitled to a free bus pass from your local authority. You can use it at any time of the day and are entitled to travel on all local bus services in Wales. The pass can also be used on some long-distance services.

Scotand: In Scotland, everyone aged 60 or over is entitled to free local bus and scheduled long-distance coach services within Scotland at any time of the day, including the morning rush hour. This scheme is run by Transport Scotland, and you need to apply for a National Entitlement Card to travel for free.

Northern Ireland: In Northern Ireland everyone aged 65 or over can travel on buses and trains for free with a Senior SmartPass.

Young Londoners

In London everyone under 16 years of age can travel free on buses and trams. This includes residents and non-residents. Children aged 14–15 will need a special photocard to take advantage of free travel. Details from www.tfl.gov.uk/tickets/faresandtickets/1063.aspx. Londoners aged 16 and 17 (and some 18-year-olds) in full-time education or on a work-based learning scheme also get free bus and tram travel.

Travel at a Discount

The easiest way for the credit-crunch savvy to travel at a discount is off-peak, as peak-time travel is the most expensive. You may be able to persuade your employer to let you come to work later and leave later so that you can travel at cheaper off-peak times. If the boss tells you the firm can't afford to give you a pay rise this year, changing your working hours and saving money on fares can give you an income increase that costs the company nothing. If off-peak is off the agenda, there are other options.

Use Discount Cards

Discount cards are available for both rail and coach services. There is a range of rail discount cards available for families, young people, the disabled, senior citizens and people living and travelling in specific areas. Not only do you get cheaper travel, but the cards often give you discounts on restaurant meals, visitor attractions, shopping and hotel rooms as well.

Cost

Most discount cards cost £24, although the Disabled Persons Railcard costs £18 and the Network card costs £20.

16–25 Railcard

This railcard is for under-25s or full-time students of any age. If you turn 26 while you hold one of the cards, renew it just before your 26th birthday anyway, even if your old card still has a month or two to run, to make sure you get another whole year's discount.

National Railcard

The website www.railcard.co.uk has details of the main national Railcard scheme. Your local railway company may have further schemes. For instance, the Devon & Cornwall card is available from First Great Western and includes discounts on buses.

Coaches

National Express coaches also has a range of coachcards for the over-60s, families, young persons and the disabled. Get details from www.nationalexpress.co.uk.

Seek out Special Deals

National Express offers £1 Funfares to a variety of destinations. Get details from the National Express website.

Mega Deals

You will also find cheap fares on Megabus for routes between major cities. Megabus also runs Megatrain services, which offer cheap rail travel between London and destinations in the South-West. Details from www.megabus.com.

Travel in a Group

There is a number of special discounts available to people travelling by rail or coach in a group.

The Friends and Family Railcard

This gives adults a third off rail travel and children 60 per cent. Up to four adults and four children can travel together using one card, and they don't have to be related. The Network Railcard gives you and up to three other adults and up to four children a third off certain off-peak fares in London and the South-East of England. Don't forget to check out 'partner' deals.

For instance, anyone buying an annual 'Gold' season ticket in the South-East rail region can get a Network railcard for just £1 for their spouse, partner or friend, which would usually cost £20.

GroupSave

This scheme offers the opportunity for three or four people to travel by rail for the price that two adults would usually pay on various off-peak ticket types. It is operated by the following companies: Chiltern Railways, National Express East Anglia, East Midlands Trains, London Midland, Southeastern, First Capital Connect, Southern, First Great Western, South West Trains, First ScotRail, London Overground, c2c.

2plus2 Coachcard

National Express's annual 2plus2 coachcard costs £16, and allows two adults paying full price to take two children free.

Rail Fares

If you don't qualify for free or discounted fares, you may still be able to travel cheaply if you buy certain tickets or travel at certain times. The website www.nationalrail.co.uk can help you to plan your train journey, but you will need to buy your ticket from one of the local train companies online, by phone or at a station, as the National Rail website doesn't actually sell tickets.

Online

You can also buy online from www.thetrainline.com and www.raileasy.co.uk, but these sites charge a booking fee, which you can avoid by booking direct from one of the train companies. It is worth registering with the Trainline, however, as it has an alerts service which tells you when the latest tranche of the cheapest tickets for your requested route go on sale. As well as the National Rail website, an excellent guide to the rail system can be found on the www.seat61.com site, run by rail enthusiast Mark Smith.

Find Your Way through the Ticket Maze

The Byzantine ticketing system previously used by the train companies, which offered scores of fares with different terms and conditions, has now been simplified into three types of fare. Anytime, Off-Peak and Advance.

Anytime

As you might expect, Anytime tickets are the most expensive as they are the most flexible, with no restrictions on when you can travel.

Off-Peak

Off-Peak fares are cheaper, to encourage you to travel when trains are less busy. Where there is more than one Off-Peak fare for a journey, the cheaper fare with more restrictions will be named Super Off-Peak.

Advance

Credit-crunch travellers will, however, be on the lookout for Advance tickets. These are single (one-way) tickets offering the cheapest rates on journeys over longer distances. As the name implies you must book your tickets in advance and travel on a specific train service.

 Get while available: The number of these tickets is limited, and when they're gone, they're gone. If you change your mind about travelling, you may be able to change the date or time of the train that the ticket is valid for, subject to availability and an administration fee, but you can't get a refund. If the administration fee is higher than the cost of the ticket, you will have to pay the difference.

 Know when: The time to look out for cheap Advance tickets is 12 weeks before your travelling date, because Network Rail must have the timetable set 12 weeks in advance, and this is usually when the cheap tickets come on the market. Alternatively, use an alert system such as the Trainline's (see opposite).

Discounts: While critics have complained that the new fare structure has eliminated some of the very cheapest tickets, the good news is that the new ticketing regime allows you to use a Railcard to get even more money off cheaper fares, which was not possible before. Child discounts apply for all Advance fares. Railcard holders get one-third off all Standard-Class Advance fares. Senior, HM Forces and Disabled Persons Railcard holders additionally get one-third off all First-Class Advance fares. Holders of the 16–25 Railcard get one-third off First-Class Advance fares for travel on CrossCountry, East Midlands Trains, First Great Western, National Express East Coast and Virgin Trains services, but tickets bought with a Railcard may be subject to a minimum fare or time restrictions.

Cheaper Tickets

There are other ways to find cheaper tickets, including not taking the most direct route and splitting up your journey into separate tickets.

Cheaper Routes

When you use a website to find the fare from one city to another, the default search is for the fastest mainline route – for instance, if you want to go to Manchester from London, you will probably be offered a route on the West Coast mainline out of Euston. However, if you use the 'via' feature – which makes the route finder seek out journeys that include a particular station – you may find a cheaper fare.

 Example: if you put 'via Kettering' into the journey finder, the London to Manchester itinerary it produces will be from St Pancras to Manchester on the Midland Mainline route, via either Nottingham or Sheffield. The journey will take a little longer, but you can save pounds travelling this way if your main objective is finding the cheapest ticket rather than the fastest journey time.

Split Your Journey

Another way to find cheaper tickets is to split your journey, and buy more than one ticket for each leg. You can then take advantage of discounted fares on part of the journey that are not available for the full trip.

- **Work it out**: First, you need to find the principal stations on the route where the train stops. You then need to find the fares for portions of the journey, and add them together to see if the total fare is cheaper than buying one ticket for the entire route. This may require some trial and error.

- **Example**: A train leaving Paddington and heading for Penzance will probably stop at Bristol, Exeter and Plymouth. By seeking out tickets from Paddington to Bristol, then Bristol to Penzance, and Paddington to Plymouth and Plymouth to Penzance, you soon discover that breaking the journey at Plymouth gives you a cheaper fare. This does not mean that you physically break your journey – you remain on the train, as you would do if you had bought just one ticket. You do, however, have two separate tickets for each part of the trip.

- **Example**: The cheapest ticket from Cheltenham to Edinburgh costs £15.50 one way with an Advance ticket, but if you've missed out on getting one of the allocated Advance tickets, you don't need to buy a full-price single, which costs £97. Simply split your journey at Wolverhampton and pay £7 for the journey from Cheltenham to Wolverhampton and £18 for the ticket from Wolverhampton to Edinburgh – giving you a magnificent saving of £72.

- **Bonus**: An even greater advantage of using split tickets is that, if you need to travel in peak time, you need only pay the peak price for the bit of the journey that takes place in peak time and not the whole journey. Pay full fare for the first bit, then take advantage of an Advance fare or a fare using a Railcard for the remainder.

Sleeper Dreams

If you need to travel between London and Scotland, consider using the Caledonian Sleeper, which travels each way every night except Saturday night. The sleeper trains travel between London and towns and cities all over Scotland, with the cost of berths starting at a special budget price of £19. More details from www.firstscotrail.com. Sleeper trains also operate on the London to Penzance route. Prices for a berth start at £34 plus the cost of the train ticket. That doesn't sound so cheap, but consider that you will be asleep, and therefore not buying snacks – or indeed paying for a hotel room if you want to break your journey. To book rail tickets and reserve sleepers, simply visit any main rail station or book by phone using most credit and debit cards. First ScotRail: 08457 550033; First Great Western 0845 700 0125.

More Ways to Cut Rail Travel Costs

Rover's Return

If you intend to travel a great deal in a particular area over a limited time – perhaps during a holiday – it is worth checking out Rail Rovers and Rail Rangers, which give unlimited travel over all or selected parts of the UK network. You can get more information about these options from www.nationalrail.co.uk/promotions.

Reclaim Your Fare If the Train Is Delayed

If the train is delayed for more than 30 minutes, you may be entitled to a refund of your fare. If you are delayed, ask for a claim form at your station, and remember to keep your ticket to prove which train you were on.

The Right Bite

Apply for a Bite card at www.bitecard.co.uk, and save 20 per cent on food and snacks at 13 different outlets at UK railway stations.

Travelling Further Afield: Flights and Ferries

Much of the information on travelling cheaply by air is covered in the Holidays section of this book (pages 180–203), but if you need to travel within the UK or on business it is worth noting a few tips and tricks.

Flights

Get Free (or Heavily Discounted) Flights

To fly for free or at bargain rates, sign up as a courier. Couriers carry valuable documents or accompany cargo. Bear in mind that you may need to travel without luggage, or without hand baggage, because the consignment takes up your allowance. You also need to be flexible about when you travel, as you will be fitting in with the client's timetable and you will usually travel alone. If you are able to travel with a companion they will have to pay the full fare. Check out the International Association of Air Travel Couriers www.courier.org (membership costs $50), www.couriertravel.org and www.aircourier.co.uk for opportunities.

No Luggage, No Food

For short-haul, short-stay flights, such as day-return business trips, choose an airline that charges extra for hold luggage and in-flight meals — and save money by declining both options.

Frequent Flyers

If you use a certain airline regularly, sign up for their frequent flyer programme and get cheaper flights or preferential treatment on future flights. As well as the airlines' own frequent flyer schemes, AirMiles can be collected at many outlets, including Tesco, where Tesco Clubcard vouchers can be exchanged for AirMiles.

Timing Is Everything for the Best Deals on Flights

When buying flights be mindful of what time of day you book and on what day of the week. Many online booking services for budget airlines hike prices at the end of the week and at weekends – look on Monday Tuesday and Wednesday for the best prices. Also avoid booking at lunchtimes and early evenings, when prices also rise to take account of the extra interest from potential customers at these times.

Ferry Good Prices

The website www.day-tripper.net offers ferry deals from £20 a head, or Eurotunnel for £49 per car. Despite the high exchange rate for the euro, these deals mean that it is still worthwhile making a day trip to France to stock up on wine and groceries.

Drive down the Cost of Motoring

Cars are more than just a form of transport. Our choice of car says a lot about our personality: flashy and flamboyant, say, or solid and reliable. They also reflect our stage in life: are we carefree and single, family-oriented, or enjoying our later years? How often does a lottery winner or other lucky windfall recipient say that they are going to buy a new car? A fine car is a symbol of being well-to-do and successful, expense no object. But the cost of driving is accelerating faster than a Maserati up an empty motorway. OK, so you can't give up the car. But you could still save money by considering a few options.

Choosing a Car

If you have to have a car, at least make sure you get the best deal on the best vehicle for you.

Cash or Car?

If you are offered a company car – on which you will have to pay tax – or a cash alternative, find out which is the most advantageous for you by using the calculators at www.cashorcar.co.uk. If you opt for a company car, make sure that you choose one that has low CO_2 emissions. The tax you pay will vary between 10 and 35 per cent of the car's list price, depending on how fuel-efficient the car is.

Trade down

Gas-guzzlers are yesterday's cars. If you have a big, thirsty car, trade down to something smaller and more fuel-efficient.

Get More Miles per Gallon

If you want to get more miles per gallon, you probably – though not necessarily – need to plump for a smaller engine. Generally speaking, the lower the cc, the better the fuel efficiency. There are, however, exceptions. Cars with good fuel economy need not necessarily be small or low-powered. Fuel efficiency can vary by as much as 30 per cent within a vehicle class. A more useful guide is the size of the car: the smaller the mass that has to be propelled, the better the fuel economy. In terms of miles per gallon, or per litre, diesel comes out ahead of petrol. Average: According to figures from the Society of Motor Manufacturers and Traders (SMMT), the average fuel economy of new petrol cars is approximately 39 mpg (7.2 litres/100 km), and for new diesel cars it is 45 mpg (6.2 litres/100 km). However, the actual range varies between 69 mpg (4.1 litres/100 km) for the most fuel-efficient small diesel Citycar and 18 mpg (16.0 litres/100 km) for one of the least fuel-efficient 'Chelsea tractors', and how you drive can be more important than what you drive (see separate section on how to use less petrol, pages 174–75).

Pay Less Vehicle Excise Duty

Choose a car with lower vehicle excise duty (VED), more usually called 'road tax'. This used to be charged at the same rate for all cars, but now the duty is assessed on a sliding scale depending on the amount of carbon dioxide emissions a car produces.

Alternative fuels: cars that use alternative fuels, such as bio fuels, will get a tax discount of between £15 and £20 in 2009–10 and £10 in 2010–11 – see the table on page 168.

Buy a New Car before April 2010: Do this to avoid the new 'showroom tax' of £950, to be imposed on the most-polluting vehicles in the first year.

✅ **Buy a Car Registered before March 2001**: Do this to pay on the old scale. The pre-graduated VED for cars registered before March 2001 for 2008–09 is £120 for cars of 1,549cc and below, and £185 for cars above 1,549cc (both up £5).

✅ **Buy a Car Registered before 1 January 1974**: Do this and you're exempt from paying road tax altogether. For further information on road tax and such matters, check out www.dvla.gov.uk/vehicles or www.vcacarfueldata.org.uk.

✅ **Two Wheels Are Better than Four**: Finally, consider switching to a motorcycle, as bikes with engines under 150cc pay just £15 road tax per year.

Graduated VED Bands and Rates for Cars Registered after 1 March 2001

VED band	CO_2 emissions (g/km)	2008–09[1] standard rate	CO_2 emissions (g/km)	2009–10 standard rate	first-year rate	2010–11 standard rate[4]
A	Up to 100	0	Up to 100	0	0	0
B	101–120	35	101–110	20	0	20
C	121–150	120	111–120	30	0	35
D	151–165	145	121–130	90	0	95
E	166–185	170	131–140	110	115	115
F	Over 186[2]	210	141–150	120	125	125
G	Over 186[3]	400	151–160	150	155	155
H			161–170	175	250	180
I			171–180	205	300	210
J			181–200	260	425	270
K			201–225	300	550	310
L			226–255	415	750	430
M			Over 255	440	950	455

[1] 2008–09 rates take effect from 13 March 2008.

[2] Cars registered before 23 March 2006.

[3] Cars registered on or after 23 March 2006.

[4] Alternative fuel car discount: 2009–10 £20 bands A–I, £15 bands J–M; 2010–11 £10 all cars.

Green Cars

If you still decide on a new car, you need to choose one that uses less fuel and with carbon dioxide emissions in the lower bands. If you go for the Goingreen G-Wiz, Volkswagen Polo BlueMotion or Seat Ibiza Ecomotive, you won't have to pay any VED at all.

Avoid Charges

There may be other advantages to a having a low-rated car. Vehicles using gas, electric power, fuel cells and bi fuel or dual fuel are exempt from paying the London congestion charge, a toll of £8 a day on cars entering central London. To qualify as exempt, they must be approved vehicles that have been converted by an approved supplier, as listed on the Transport Energy Powershift Register.

Buy Your Tax Disc Annually

If you do need to pay tax, buy an annual disc rather than a six-month one, and save money. If you buy online, you will also save on postage or time spent queuing up at the Post Office.

Hints on Buying a Car

When it comes to buying a car, have a look at *What Car?* magazine (www.whatcar.co.uk), or *Auto Trader* (www.autotrader.co.uk), which offer pages of information, including where to get the best deal and how much certain models depreciate.

Set Yourself a Budget and Stick to It

Research a car thoroughly before buying by looking at new and used car ads to find out the model's going price, so that you don't overpay.

Get a Vehicle Data Check

If you are buying a used car, get a data check for £5 from www.rac.co.uk/web/vehicle-checks, to find out whether it has finance outstanding on it or if it has been written off, scrapped or stolen.

Buy Online

According to research by *Which?* magazine, you can save an average of £3,000 when buying online. The world's largest car supermarket www.cargiant.co.uk, stocks up to 6,000 new and used cars of all makes and models – many of them cheaper than dealerships.

Don't Use Forecourt Finance

Not researching which type of finance options are the most suitable, and not comparing annualized percentage rates (APRs), costs motorists dear. According to research by insurer esure, as many as one in seven motorists take out the dealer finance offered by their car salesman, while a horrifying one in twenty or so use a credit card. This can be an expensive choice. The average cost of forecourt finance is 10.17 per cent, compared with a personal loan rate which starts at 7.4% typical APR, while credit card rates can be as high as 20 per cent.

Save Money on Insurance

Price-comparison websites such as www.gocompare.com, www.confused.com or www.tescocompare.com will help you to find the cheapest car insurance.

Use More than One Website to Compare

Beware of using just a single comparison site, however. A report by the consumer organization Which? found that consumers needed to use a variety of price-comparison sites to make sure they were getting the best deals, as well as getting quotes directly from insurers themselves. The differences in price between the various sites can be accounted for in several ways, including different questions asked by the sites when seeking out appropriate cover, and commission rates negotiated by the sites, which could result in different results appearing as best buys. Insurers worth considering, in addition to the price-comparison sites, include:

- www.admiral.com
- www.budgetinsurance.com
- www.elephant.com
- www.hastingsdirect.com
- www.norwichunion.com
- www.postoffice.co.uk
- www.swiftcover.com
- www.zurichinsurance.com

Haggle

Use quotes from a price-comparison site to haggle with your current insurer to try to get a better deal.

Seek out a Specialist

If you fall into a certain group, such as 'lady driver', 'over-50' or 'classic car owner', try a specialist insurer for your group, such as Sheilas' Wheels (www.sheilaswheels.com); Age Concern (www.ageconcern.org.uk) or Adrian Flux (www.adrianflux.co.uk), respectively.

Elastic Bands

Cars insured in the UK are allocated to one of 20 bands or 'groups', which class together cars with similar characteristics. The lower the group number, the less you will pay, so if you are buying a new car consider choosing one in a lower group. You can find out which insurance band a car falls into on the website www.parkers.co.uk/insurance.

The Association of British Insurers is currently working on a new system that splits cars into 50 groups instead of 20, which will initially run alongside the old system. Cars have been reassessed to include factors such as the damage they might do to other cars and the repairs to them that might be needed, as well as the repairs to the insured car. If you are buying a new car, and want to know where it will sit under the new system, have a look at www.thatcham.org/abigrouprating.

Put Your Partner on Your Policy

When asking for quotes ask for two – one with and one without your partner named as second driver. Naming a partner on your policy can actually work out cheaper, even if you each have your own policies anyway.

Multi Savings

If you have more than one car in the family, see if you can get a discount with a 'multicar' policy. Direct Line and Tesco offer a discount of 10 per cent on the second car, while Admiral offers up to 25 per cent.

Don't Forget Breakdown Cover

Paying for a mechanic to rescue you from the side of the motorway can be costly, so skimping on breakdown and roadside rescue cover could be a false economy. Free AA or RAC membership is often included in new car deals, but there are other suppliers to choose from if you have to buy it yourself, including Green Flag, More Than, Mondial, Direct Line, Europ Assistance, Britannia and Tesco. The www.breakdowncoveruk.co.uk website will help you to choose. If you already have breakdown cover, you may be able to obtain membership more cheaply by rejoining as a new member rather than simply renewing your membership.

Save Money Once You Are Insured

Drive within the speed limit. Tickets for speeding don't just cost you in terms of a fine and points on your licence, they also add an average of 13 per cent to insurance premiums.

Drive Carefully

If you never have an accident, you could end up with a no-claims discount of as much as 70 per cent. All the more incentive to drive carefully.

Protect Your No-Claims Bonus

Get a protected no-claims bonus once you qualify for it, as you won't lose your bonus if you make a claim.

Buy Third-Party Cover

If you own a low-value car, buying third-party cover only will save you money.

Take the Pass Plus

If you are a new driver, take the Pass Plus test and save money on your insurance. This is a supplementary driving course for new drivers. Although you will have to pay for the course, which will take a minimum of six hours, you will be eligible for discounts offered by insurance companies which recognize the scheme. The amount you save will depend on the insurer, but you may even save more than you paid out for the course.

Use Less Petrol

First of all, avoid using your car at all for short journeys – use public transport, ride a bicycle or walk. If you must use the car, being fuel-efficient is one of the easiest ways you can save on the cost of motoring, not to mention the ecological benefit.

Travel Light

Remove unnecessary junk from your boot. The extra weight of unused golf clubs, tool kits and other bits and pieces makes cars less aerodynamic, and that means higher petrol consumption. Also, don't fill up the tank. The extra weight of the petrol has the same effect on fuel consumption as extra luggage in the boot.

Improve on Aerodynamics

Remove redundant roof racks when not in use. Roof racks also add to the weight and impair the aerodynamic performance of a car, increasing fuel consumption by up to 30 per cent. If you don't know how to remove the roof rack, get a professional to help.

Air Con v. Drag

Avoid using air conditioning. Air conditioners' compressors increase the load on the engine, and that in turn increases your car's fuel consumption. Open the windows instead – even if it does increase drag. If you don't need the window or sunroof open, close them because of the increase in drag.

Tyre Pressure

Ensure that your tyres are at the correct pressure. A recent US government report found that 1.2bn (US) gallons of fuel are wasted annually as a result of underinflated tyres. Overinflated tyres can be dangerous, so it is important to maintain your tyres at the correct pressure.

Plan Your Route

Planning ahead can enable you to miss the rush hour and busy roads, so that you can maintain a constant cruising speed and avoid constant braking and accelerating. Knowing exactly where you are going also means that you don't have to keep slowing down to look for turn-offs, or turning back when you find you've taken the wrong road.

Drive Smoothly

Cut your speed on motorways, as higher speeds use more fuel. There is no need to rev up at traffic lights – this burns fuel unnecessarily, as well as increasing CO_2 emissions. Try to keep your engine revs between 1,500 and 2,500 rpm. Move off gently, reach your optimum speed smoothly and maintain this speed for maximum miles per gallon. Accelerating fiercely eats up excessive fuel at once.

Gears and Engine

Change gears only when you need to. Racing the engine in a low gear could add 25 per cent to the cost of filling the tank. Avoid letting the engine warm up before you drive off, as it wastes fuel. Drive gently for the first few minutes instead, until the engine warms.

Savings When Buying Petrol

Do not assume that petrol prices are the same everywhere – it pays to shop around and look for deals. For example, try to avoid filling up at motorway services, as they usually charge higher prices than other locations.

Source Cheaper Prices Online

Check online for the cheapest petrol in your region. The website www.petrolprices.com gives details of where to fill up for less in your area.

Seek out Supermarket Promotions

Supermarkets such as Sainsbury's and Tesco often run promotions giving you money off fuel if you spend a certain amount on your shopping in-store. Take advantage of cards such as Morrisons Miles, which are linked to grocery shopping.

Pay for Petrol with a Cashback Card

See pages 79–80 for details of cashback cards – but remember, use a cashback card only if you pay your credit card bill in full every month. The higher interest rates associated with cashback cards will cost you money compared with using another card unless you clear the debt completely every month.

Rewards Schemes

If you don't have a cashback card, look out for other reward schemes, such as Tesco Clubcard, which gives you points for buying fuel. Shell and Asda both offer discounts if you pay with their own credit cards.

Other Motoring Savings

Buy Tyres Online

If you need new tyres, check out www.etyres.co.uk, which charges between 10 and 15 per cent less than ordinary fitters and will send someone out to fit your new tyres. Other online tyre retailers include www.tyre-shopper.co.uk and www.mytyres.co.uk.

Don't Pay Road Tax If the Car Is off the Road

If you car is off the road for more than six months, apply for a SORN (Statutory Off Road Notification), which means you don't need to pay VED or road tax.

Pay Penalties and Charges on Time

In london, for example, you should pay a parking penalty within 14 days or find that the price has doubled. And pay the congestion charge before midnight on the charging day following your journey. This means you avoid a £120 penalty charge notice.

Carry a Passenger

There are plans for up to 500 miles (800 km) of car-sharing lanes on motorways, and you will also be able to use the scheme currently in force on the Leeds–Bradford link road in Yorkshire. You will save money on fuel by not being held up in traffic, as well as getting to your destination faster.

Car Sharing

Also known as lift sharing, ride sharing and car pooling, this is an extension of the carry-a-passenger idea, and encourages drivers not to travel alone. Car sharers save money on motoring costs, save time looking for parking spaces and help to save the planet by reducing carbon footprints.

☑ **Colleagues**: You may be able to find a car-share partner at your place of work, and arrange between yourselves whether you are always to use the same car or alternate with the driving. Companies with an eco-friendly transport policy will encourage employees to share transport, and set up schemes to match sharers.

☑ **Schemes**: If you can't find a sharer from among your colleagues and friends, there are several national schemes which put you in contact with others and suggest how it should be done. There is a directory of car-sharing sites on www.carshare.com, and more information can be found on www.nationalcarshare.co.uk, www.liftshare.org and www.liftsharesolutions.com.

Car Clubs

If you like to drive, but don't want the expense of owning your own car, you can either rent when you need a car – for instance, when you go on holiday – or, if you occasionally just need to nip down the road and don't want to take the bus, join a car club. A car club is essentially a fleet of pool cars available to all members. It gives you the freedom of having access to a car without actually owning one. You get to drive a car when you need to, but you can forget about car loans, road tax, insurance, service bills, depreciation, parking permits, cleaning and even fuel.

☑ **Type of cars**: Cars are usually new, low-emission vehicles, and you pay only for the time you actually use them. Vehicles are located in specially designated car club bays and are collected from these bays, and returned to them after use.

☑ **Examples**: Two of the major players are Streetcar (Streetcar.co.uk) and Whizzgo (whizzgo.co.uk). Others include City Car Club (citycarclub.co.uk) and Zipcar (Zipcar.co.uk).

✓ **Rates**: The standard rate for car clubs is around £5 an hour. Both Whizzgo and Streetcar have an annual membership charge of £49.50. Streetcar's hourly rates start at £3.95 for an introductory offer. While Whizzgo offers a variety of packages starting at £50 a month, it also offers pay-as-you-go starting at £5.15 an hour. Most car club cars in London are exempt from the congestion charge. The cost includes fuel, insurance, cleaning, servicing, maintenance, repair and breakdown costs.

✓ **How it works**: You can book a car quickly and conveniently online or by phone: for an hour, a day or as long as you like. When you sign up to the scheme, you are given a smart card and PIN number. You pick your car up from the designated parking place, open the car with the smart card, enter your PIN to release the keys, start the car and off you go. When your time is up, you return the car. If you find you need the car for longer, if no one else has booked it you use the in-car radio to extend the booking.

Car Hire

Shop around if you are hiring a car, and consider taking separate insurance from the one offered by the hire company. The website www.insurance4carhire.com can help you to choose.

Keep Your Car Properly Maintained

Take care of your car, and have it serviced regularly.

Wash Your Car Yourself

Avoid paying for a car wash – use a bucket of water containing car shampoo, and use a sponge. Rinse with a hose, and polish with a chamois. Avoid using washing-up liquid, which could damage the paintwork and leave out the hosedown if you have a water meter, to save money on the water bill.

Holidays

Stay in the UK

Everyone needs a holiday. Escaping the stresses of your daily life is essential, as is taking the time out to relax and recharge your batteries fairly regularly. But you don't need to spend a fortune to have a great time. Taking a holiday in Britain means cutting down on flying costs and discovering some of the great attractions that we have in the UK. The main downside? The weather, of course! If you're worried about the weather, you can check the five-day forecast at www.bbc.co.uk/weather/5day.shtml. Simply set the search for the area of your choice.

Stay at Home

There couldn't be a cheaper holiday than staying at home. There are no accommodation or travel costs, for starters. And with a little bit of research, you may discover you have lots of fun and interesting sights to see and things to do locally.

Research Your Area

First pop in to the local library to borrow any guide books for your area. Check first the free attractions, such as houses, parks, ports and so on. A family can spend many happy and inexpensive hours exploring and discovering the sights of their own area. And there could be plenty of hidden delights, which are a joy to find. Also, while you're at the library, check out local listings magazines or newspapers for up-to-the-minute news of free or cheap activities and events. With some planning, it's quite possible to pack in a week's worth of fun days out at very little cost.

Fun at the Park

Picnics at the park, for instance, can be livened up by a softball tournament or treasure hunt.

Museums

London's main museums – the National History, Science and British museums, for instance – all have free entry, and can offer hours of interesting entertainment. Get other families involved for more fun.

Deals

Look for vouchers and ways to get cheap entry to some of the UK's top attractions. Tesco's website, for instance, swaps Clubcard vouchers for days out. For example, normal adult entry to Alton Towers is £34 – but with Tesco vouchers sorted out in advance at www.tesco.com, it's just £8.50. You could also try www.lastminute.com, which offers deals not only on holidays, but for days out at top attractions, theatre tickets, spas and restaurants too. Alternatively, go to www.daysoutuk.com, where you can search more than 7,000 attractions and 300 discount vouchers for great days out, attractions, theme parks, places to go and fun things to do across the UK and Ireland.

Getting Away

Sometimes you just need to get away from the house and the area where you spend your day-to-day life – it might not matter too much to you *where* you go, as long as you don't stay at home. You can, however, have a great UK break on a budget.

Cheap UK Hotels

Most of the large hotel chains do regular special offers, such as two-nights-for-the-price-of-one, free meals or spa access and treatments. Register at the hotel's website to get deal alerts sent to your inbox.

Hotel updates: Travelodge, for instance, sends out regular email updates of its offers across its chain. Register at www.travelodge.co.uk. The Holiday Inn chain offers a similar service, which you can sign up for at www.ichotelsgroup.com.

Websites: There are also numerous sites that search hotel deals to bring you the lowest prices. For instance, www.halfpricehotels.co.uk tries to find the best hotel offers in England, Scotland, Wales and Ireland, while www.laterooms.com promises to find cheap hotels, discount hotels and last-minute hotel deals.

B&Bs: Don't forget to look at available B&Bs. Many offer excellent accommodation at fractions of the cost of a hotel room. Go to www.bedandbreakfasts.co.uk or www.enjoyengland.com for a choice of B&Bs around the country.

Alternatives: If you fancy trying alternative accommodation, such as a barn or bunkhouse, to save money, try www.yha.org.uk for a relatively cheap and unusual holiday. Out of term time there are lots of available cheap rooms in university halls of residence. Many are listed at www.travelstay.com, which also sources cheap hotels and hostel accommodation in the UK.

Self-Catering

Self-catering holidays can work out considerably cheaper than staying in swanky hotels. You get the added benefit of choosing your own menus and producing meals at reasonable prices, rather than paying hotel mark-ups. There are thousands of delightful cottages for hire around the country, many within walking distance of beaches or moors, and so ideal for holidays. Unbooked cottages are often reduced a week or two before their empty period, which means that you can often pick up a bargain at the last minute.

There is also a range of hostels, which can be a lot cheaper than hotels. Despite their reputation, many hostels are clean and friendly, with free Internet access and breakfast. Try the following:

- **www.english-country-cottages.co.uk** – for around 3,000 cottages
- **www.welcomecottages.com** – for around 2,000 properties
- **www.cottages4you.co.uk**
- **www.country-holidays.co.uk**
- **www.yha.org.uk** – for prices and availability of youth hostels
- **www.hosteluk.com**
- **www.backpackers.co.uk**

Camp

If you are already a fan of camping, you know how cheap and fun it can be. If you haven't camped before, get some advice on what kit you need. A decent tent is a must, plus groundsheets and sleeping bags.

- **When to buy**: It's a good idea to buy your camping stuff out of season in the autumn/winter, when it is usually reduced in price.

- **Advice**: There are plenty of forums and discussion areas online where you can get advice on what camping equipment you will need, but you should also check out the following for tips and hints on campsites: www.ukcampsite.co.uk and www.myfavouritecampsite.com.

- **Camping club**: Before setting off, it's a good idea to join the Camping & Caravanning Club at www.campingandcaravanningclub.co.uk. It costs £35 – plus a £7 joining fee for the first year – but you should get that back in savings in your first few nights. As a member you'll get reductions on campsite fees, and some of their holiday sites are attached to commercial sites, so you can use their facilities very cheaply.

Heading Abroad?

If you're a real sun seeker, then you'll have to head overseas to find decent weather. But by avoiding the tourist hot spots, you could get a great beach holiday at much lower prices. There are thousands of miles of beautiful beaches in the world, and only a small percentage of them are in hot spots such as Spain and Greece.

Planning

The more you plan your holiday, the more money you can save. Timing can be crucial, as can getting local knowledge from the destination of your choice. If you're flying to the US, for instance, it's worth talking direct to the American tour operators as well as UK ones. Local airlines and tour operators will often offer the cheaper deals, and the local tourist office can send you lists of B&Bs and other accommodation that wouldn't make it into tour operator brochures. You'll also find friends, family and work colleagues a great source for tips and hints for different destinations. Everyone likes sharing the knowledge they've built about different places around the world.

Destination

Consider lesser-known destinations such as Gambia and Cape Verde to save money. If you can really take the heat, there are often sensational summer deals in very hot countries such as Dubai – however, you'll need to take lots of suncream because it's scorching and few people are comfortable in such heat! If you can still find a cheap return flight to the US – in spite of the recent rises in fuel charges – it might be a good destination to choose bearing in mind the weak dollar, which has meant the same goods at almost half the price in US stores.

All-Inclusive

Booking an all-inclusive package deal can be a good idea when fuel costs are rising and there are unpredictable exchange rates. An all-inclusive holiday means that you'll know how much you're spending before you go. Otherwise you could discover that prices at your resort have rocketed, as well as fuel prices increased.

Booking Early

The timing of your booking is crucial to get the best bargains. You should either wait until the last minute – which is very risky – or book really, *really* early. Book as soon as the tour brochures come out – which can be nine months before your holiday – to get early booking discounts of around £100 per couple, or buy-one-week-get-one-week-free deals.

Booking at the Last Minute

Leave it really, really late, and you may get cheaper holidays. But leaving it late usually means a very limited choice. You should start looking at late deals around eight weeks before your planned departure. Bear in mind that the later you can leave it, the more desperate holiday companies are to flog empty rooms, so the price drops further. If you need crèche facilities or want particular resorts or hotels, leaving it late is not a good idea. But if you aren't too fussy about where you go and just want some sun and sand, you could end up with a great deal.

 Call direct: It's often worth calling hotels direct and asking if they have any empty rooms. If they say yes, ask if they can offer you a last-minute rate. They would probably rather have you in the room at a reduced price than be left with an empty room, so it may be possible to pick up a massive discount.

Teletext: For last-minute bargains, www.teletext.co.uk can be a great resource. Or you can use the prices you see on Teletext to haggle with other holiday firms.

Timing: The timing of your holiday can also be crucial in saving money. Take a holiday when others can't, and the prices are cheaper. For instance, family destinations such as Florida are much cheaper before school holidays in May and June. Try to avoid travelling on a Saturday. Leaving on a Sunday instead of a Saturday can cut your travel costs by half, not to mention remove the hassle of fighting big crowds. Holidays from Tuesday to Tuesday can also yield savings of as much as £100 per person.

Passport

Check that your passport is valid and won't run out while you're away. If there could be a problem, make sure that you apply for your passport in plenty of time. It will not only mean avoiding worry, but could also mean making a cash saving. Passports are not cheap these days, but leave it to the last minute and you'll be asked for more than £100. In fact the Passport

Service's same-day premium service costs a whopping £114 for the renewal of a passport. The next quickest service takes a week, so if you're five working days from your trip and discover you need a new passport, you'll have to pay the top rate. A replacement passport delivered in a week costs £97. The two-week check-and-send service available at Post Offices costs £72, plus a £7 fee to the Post Office. The standard passport service, which takes a minimum of three weeks – or much longer in busy times, such as immediately before summer – costs £72. If you're sensible, you'll check now to save paying up to £42 extra for a new passport.

Packing

There's one simple rule about packing these days: pack light. Airlines are trying to recoup the cost of cheaper tickets by charging much more for stowed luggage. You can avoid the extra charges altogether by restricting yourself to a carry-on bag. You'll also avoid the misery of lost luggage in the process. Ryanair, for instance, charges £7.50 for every bag you need to store in the hold, although you can halve the cost by pre-booking online.

 Weight: Be aware of baggage weight limits. Ryanair, again, only allows bags of up to 15kg in weight. Extra kilograms are charged at £5.50 per kg.

Number: And be aware of bag limits. If you have more than one bag per person, you'll be charged heavily for the extra bags. British Airways, for example, charges £120 for every extra bag you take on long-haul flights. The charge falls to £60 on short-haul flights and £30 on domestic flights.

Travel Money

Don't get stung exchanging currency – save money by sorting out your holiday finance before you leave. Leave it until the last minute, and you will end up paying more for your money. You could be hit by transaction charges, foreign exchange fees – or simple rip-off rates offered abroad.

Online

Order your holiday cash online to get discounts. With Travelex, for instance, you can pick up cash ordered more cheaply online at one of their airport shops.

Banks

Alternatively, you can pre-order holiday money through your bank or building society – but be wary of delivery charges of up to a fiver.

Credit Cards

If you plan to use a credit card abroad, check the fees. Anyone planning to buy with a credit card should get plastic from the Post Office, Nationwide or Saga. Their cards don't levy foreign exchange fees in Europe, which can add three per cent to your credit card charge.

Check Your Account

If you have a special bank account such as a student account, graduate account or monthly fee account, you may get fee-free foreign exchange as part of your package. Having commission waived will almost certainly give you a better rate than using a 'commission-free' service.

Travel Insurance

Don't take out travel insurance from your travel agent. Do it separately online or through a broker, and it will be cheaper. If you are likely to travel again within 12 months, it's probably cheaper to buy a year's cover.

Using Your Phone Abroad

The best advice is to leave your phone behind and save pounds. But it's hard for most people to give up their mobile habit, even when abroad, so it's important to check out the cost before gaily chatting away, thinking that you'll be charged at your usual rate.

Eurotariff

There's a Eurotariff which limits the amount you can be charged when making calls abroad. But it is still steep. You can be charged up to 49 euro cents a minute – which works out at around 38p a minute – to make a call when in Europe. But the sting comes when someone calls you. You'll be charged up to 24 euro cents a minute – around 19p a minute – to receive a call.

International SIM Cards

The solution is to get a local or international SIM card. International SIM cards cost around £30, but mean that you will be able to receive calls while abroad without having to pay for them, which can mean saving tens of pounds. They also may be cheaper than your UK phone provider when it comes to making calls or sending texts from abroad. You can order an international SIM card from www.gosim.com, www.sim4travel.com or www.globalsimcard.co.uk.

Voicemail

Here's a good tip – switch off your voicemail before you leave the UK. You'll be charged every time someone leaves you a message, then charged again every time you call your voicemail from abroad otherwise.

Phonecards

If you simply want to be able to call home from time to time, then it will work out cheaper to get an international phonecard. They're freely available from places such as the Post Office. Once overseas, you simply need to find a public phone to make your call.

Accommodation

Open your mind to the many kinds of accommodation on offer – comfortable rooms of a decent standard can be had outside of the usual hotels.

Cheap Hotels

The Internet has made it easy to find cheap or reduced-price hotel deals. There are several well-established sites that offer to find deals for you. Try www.lastminute.com, www.expedia.co.uk

or www.ebookers.com for hundreds of hotels from all over the world. If you have already decided your destination, www.traveljungle.co.uk has a more detailed search system and a better selection of hotels. To save wasting time looking at luxury hotels well outside your price range, go to www.priceline.co.uk, where you can name your price and destination, and the site will find a hotel that you can afford.

Hostels

Hostels abroad can be a decent cheap alternative, and many have decent rooms and facilities. You don't even need to risk getting a bad one. Go to www.hostelbookers.com or www.hostelworld.com to read reviews by other travellers. Both sites give hostels a percentage rating, based on users' experiences. Both also allow you to book your rooms. Another tip – if you're planning to stay at a Hostelling International hostel, you can get £3 a night off by joining the Youth Hostel Association for £16. Go to www.yha.org.uk.

B&Bs

Don't overlook B&Bs in Europe and the US. French and Italian bed and breakfasts, in particular, are usually of a really high standard and are often the homes of the proprietors.

Rental

Another alternative is to rent properties direct from their owners. People advertise their places on websites such as www.gumtree.com or www.craigslist.co.uk, which both have sites for different cities around the world, including the UK.

Student Websites

You may not be a student, but a lot of sites aimed at student travellers offer fantastic travel bargains that can be used by others. The hotels and tours that they offer are targeted at student travellers on a tight budget, which obviously means saving money. But they are also usually of a good standard, so tend to be clean, cheap and safe. It's a particularly good idea for more exotic locations. Go to www.adventurecompany.co.uk or www.statravel.co.uk for some ideas.

 Volunteer: If you want to take a longer break, become a volunteer. You will have to contribute in some way, so it will be a working holiday, but the rewards can be tremendous. There are plenty of volunteer projects around the world looking for your help for anything from as short as three weeks to 12 months or longer.

 **Summer job**: If you have a summer free and want to travel, you could get a job at a summer camp. You'll usually have to find your own air fare, but you will have accommodation for free and be fed and paid.

House Swap and Staying at People's Homes

Are you comfortable with the idea of strangers staying in your home? If so, a house swap could be right up your street. There are lots of home-swapping sites where you can be introduced to people all over the world who want to swap homes with someone elsewhere in the world. You have to offer your own home as an exchange and find someone who wants to visit it. You can register for free at www.homexchangevacation.com, or try www.homebase-hols.com or www.homelink.org.uk.

Location: City dwellers should not have much problem finding a prospective swapper, but other areas of the country may find it a little harder – although there are plenty of people who would jump at the chance to stay in a remote cottage or seaside terrace, for instance.

Accommodation type: You need to be realistic when sorting out a swap. If you have a two-bedroom flat, for instance, you shouldn't expect to swap it for a 12-bedroom mansion. But you should be able to find an equivalent property to yours somewhere.

How to: Go to one of the websites, and pick your destination to see whether there are any suitable properties available. You will need to talk to the swapper and arrange the details of your exchange. It's essential to set some ground rules as to what you have available in your home and let your visitors know what restrictions you want to impose. If you can come to an agreement, you should both end up with a much cheaper holiday in a decent property.

Alternative: Another option is to sleep on people's sofas around the world – which is really only practical for single people. You have to agree to let others sleep on your sofa. Go to www.couchsurfing.com for more details. Another site offering a similar service is www.airbedandbreakfast.com, where people rent out everything from spare rooms to an airbed on their floor.

Holiday Transport

You may not have a choice about how you travel to the airport or your UK destination, but if you do have the option it's worth looking at alternatives. A coach could be the cheapest way to get there but, if you book early enough, a train could work out only slightly more expensive. If you're driving, it's crucial to find ways to cut the cost of petrol and parking. Then there's the cost of flights.

Take the Train

Book your train tickets to the airport as soon as you've booked your flights or package holiday, and you'll make considerable savings.

Advance Booking

Super Apex offer the lowest fares – substantially cheaper than returns bought on the day – but must be booked at least two weeks in advance. Visit either www.networkrail.co.uk or www.thetrainline.com, where you'll be able to take advantage of early booked savers. You can also sign up for Ticket Alerts via www.thetrainline.com, which will notify you, by email, when advanced tickets become available. The service could help you to make decent cost savings.

Two Singles

Don't automatically get a return ticket. Sometimes getting two singles can work out cheaper. Consumer magazine *Which Money?* recently discovered that a Saver Return ticket from Southampton to Cardiff over a weekend cost £35. But two singles were only £7 each – a saving of more than £20.

Railcard

Get a Family and Friends Railcard to cut the price of train tickets even further. Go to www.familyandfriends-railcard.co.uk to apply for your card – which will give you up to third off ticket prices for adults, or 60 per cent off for kids. It costs just £24 for a year – or £65 for three years – and you could save that much on just one journey, as up to four adults and four kids can travel on the one Railcard.

Off-Peak

If you can travel at off-peak times, you'll pay lower fares on trains and buses. Plan your journey to travel on the first off-peak train or bus to save pounds.

Airport Trains

Don't rush to get so-called airport express train services. They work out a lot more expensive than scheduled services and are usually only a few minutes faster. The Gatwick Express to and from London's Victoria station, for instance, costs £16.90 each way. But you could buy a return on the Southern Rail service from Victoria to Gatwick for just £17. The journey takes five minutes longer, but is almost half the price!

Take the Coach

Travelling to your airport by coach can be much cheaper than letting the train take the strain. A return ticket from Edinburgh to London on the train, for instance, could be around £100. By coach it's around £40 – a 60 per cent saving. However, the coach can take much longer – twice as long as the train in that Edinburgh example.

Annual Pass

You can cut the cost of coach travel by getting an annual pass. National Express has a 2plus2 annual family pass for £16 a year, which allows two full paying adults to take two children for free. If it's just you and one child, they also do a 1plus1 deal on the same basis. You can book coach tickets and apply for an annual pass online at www.nationalexpress.com.

Taking the Car

If you're driving to the airport, there are a few ways you can keep the cost down.

Petrol

Buy the cheapest petrol you can. Go to www.petrolprices.com to find the cheapest petrol prices in your area. You could be surprised at the difference. Drive more slowly – driving at 80 km/h (50 mph) instead of 110 km/h (70 mph) can cut your fuel bill by 30 per cent.

Parking

If you need to park at an airport, book ahead online to get discounts of up to 60 per cent. Go to www.gosimply.com/airport-parking, which compares rates at all major UK airports. Or find cheaper alternatives to expensive airport parking:

- **Spare driveways**: Go to www.parkatmyhouse.com, where people rent out empty driveways or parking spaces. The price you pay is agreed between you and the person renting out their space.

- **Meet and greet**: With this service someone meets you at the airport, then drives your car away to a secure location until your return. They will then be waiting for you at arrivals with your car keys when you return. Put 'meet and greet' and the name of the airport you're travelling from into Google to find services in the area.

Airport Hotels

If you're driving to the airport and your flight leaves very early in the morning, consider airport hotels. Most of the airport hotels have deals where the room rate is inclusive of parking for two weeks. It means you could save money and add a little bit of luxury to your trip. It may even help you to get a decent night's sleep before an early flight.

Rental

If you need to rent a car in the UK or abroad, www.carrentals.co.uk compares all the major car-hire companies to get you the best deal.

Cheap Fights

Despite rising fuel prices, cheap flights are still available if you know where to look, the Internet being the most likely source of good deals.

Websites

There is a huge selection of Internet sites where you can get information on cheap flights and holidays. Try the following:

- **www.travelzoo.co.uk**: Register here and you'll be sent a weekly email of the top 20 independent 'insider' guides to the best holidays, hotels and flight deals, many of which will save you cash.

- **www.cheapflights.co.uk**: Get bargain flights as well as competitively priced hotels and car hire.

- **www.travelsupermarket.com**: This claims to be a one-stop shop for saving money on all aspects of travel.

- **www.skyscanner.net**: This does live searches to find the best deals.

- **www.momondo.com**: A similar offering to Skyscanner.

Timing

When booking flights online, you should bear in mind that the day and time at which you book could affect prices. Avoid booking at lunchtime, weekends and early evenings when air fares tend to be at their most expensive. You're more likely to pick up a bargain if you book a flight in the middle of the afternoon or early in the morning, traditionally quiet times in the sales offices.

Shop Around

It goes without saying that you should shop around, but it's also true of comparison sites. Specialist travel sites such as www.expedia.com and www.lastminute.com are great for flight and hotel deals, but their prices vary. You may discover the same hotel or flight at a cheaper price on a rival site, so check as many as you can before booking for the best price.

Opodo

If you're booking a long-haul flight, there's a tool on travel site Opodo that tracks the prices of more than 100 major airlines to show you when prices will drop to their lowest point. Go to promos.opodo.co.uk/travel/airlines to check out the tool and possibly make savings of hundreds of pounds.

Go Directly to the Source

In fact, before booking online it's an idea to call the hotel or flight operator directly to see if they can undercut the deal. Hotels may often match or offer you cheaper rates if you ask, as it means that they don't have to pay commission to the website.

Auctions

Have you tried a travel auction? It's an opportunity to bid for holidays, hotels and air fares at whatever price you can afford. Internet auction site www.ebay.co.uk is a good place to start, and you can find travel auctions at www.priceline.com or www.skyauction.com.

Courier Flights

Find out about being an air courier, and get flights at up to a quarter of their usual price. Register with the International Association of Air Carriers at www.aircourier.co.uk to get details of couriers needed for flights going all over the world. You simply have to take charge of a package or shipping documents at one end and deliver it at the other. Companies use couriers because it is quicker to have a courier check freight through as excess baggage than it is for a firm to send freight as air cargo. Once you've signed over the freight, you're free to enjoy your holiday.

Sport & Leisure

Exercise and Sport

Regular exercise is necessary to your health as well as being fun, and it can have a long-term money-saving effect – if you're fitter and healthier, you may not need to spend so much on healthcare later on. But joining clubs and buying equipment rack up the costs. Finding ways to exercise cheaply is a worthwhile task.

Exercise for Free

Ask yourself if you really need to belong to any kind of health club or gym. It could be much easier and save you pots of cash to simply run in your nearest local park. There are also simple ways to increase the amount of exercise you do in your day-to-day life.

Walking

Walk up the stairs at work or elsewhere rather than taking the lift; get off the bus or tube a stop before your home or work, and walk the remaining distance; use local shops, and carry your groceries home rather than driving to the supermarket. In fact walk everywhere you can – you'll soon feel the benefits, and it will have cost you nothing.

Cycling

Consider cycling to work. It will not only help you get fitter, but will also save you the cost of commuting. The average Londoner, for instance, spends £150 on trains, tubes or buses to work every month. Cycling will also mean saying goodbye to the misery of commuting and waiting for buses or trains that don't arrive – or are too full when they do.

Running

It is much more pleasant and interesting to run outside than indoors at the gym. You could even consider running to work if it's not too far and you have a shower at your workplace. It's a great way to get fit quick.

Exercise for Less

Sometimes a little outlay at some stage in the process is necessary to get the kind of activity you want, but it does not have to break the bank.

Health Clubs

If you belong to an expensive health club, cancel your subscription. You're probably paying between £30 and £80 a month for membership, but council-run leisure centres cost about half that and are perfectly adequate for general swimming and circuit training.

Swimming

If you want to swim, the local public baths will be a much cheaper way of getting in a few regular lengths than at an expensive gym or leisure facility.

Create Your Own Exercise Regime

There are lots of ways to get tips on different types of exercises. There are plenty of books with good advice – and they can all be borrowed for free from the library. If the library doesn't have want you want in stock, you can ask them to order it. There is also plenty of useful advice online at www.crossfit.com. CrossFit is a strength and conditioning programme used by many police forces and military outfits. Here's their 'World-class fitness programme in 100 words':

- 'Eat meat and vegetables, nuts and seeds, some fruit, little starch and no sugar. Keep intake to levels that will support exercise but not body fat.'

- 'Practise and train major lifts: deadlift, clean, squat, presses, C&J, and snatch.'

- 'Similarly, master the basics of gymnastics: pull-ups, dips, rope climb, push-ups, sit-ups, presses to handstand, pirouettes, flips, splits, and holds.'

- 'Bike, run, swim, row hard and fast.'

- 'Five or six days per week mix these elements in as many combinations and patterns as creativity will allow.'

- 'Routine is the enemy. Keep workouts short and intense.'

- 'Regularly learn and play new sports.'

Play Football and Games at the Park

Football is an excellent way to keep fit and as much fun as you remember it. In recent times there have been hundreds of great new five-a-side centres springing up all over the country with 10 or more pitches in each location, allowing more people than ever to play and enjoy the game. But why pay out the £40 or so cost for an hour's hire of a pitch when you can play in your local park for free?

- **Goals**: If you want reasonably proper goals, you can buy foldaway ones fairly cheaply – for £10–20 at the likes of Argos.

- **Balls**: Don't be tempted to splash out on expensive replica balls. Local sports shops sell decent-enough balls for around £3.

- **Kits**: You don't even need to buy kits. Just ask one lot to wear white and the other coloured shirts. Sorted!

- **Tennis**: Most parks are also stocked with tennis courts which you can hire for an hour for a few quid, saving the cost of expensive tennis club membership fees.

- **Other games**: And there are plenty of other games you can play with a few sticks and balls. Cricket and softball, for instance, are both ideal games to play at the park and don't need much in the way of special equipment.

Join With Others

Some sports and hobbies simply require you to spend money. You can't play golf, for instance, without a set of clubs. It is, in fact, one of the most expensive hobbies to have. According to recent research from the Yorkshire Bank, Britain's golfers spend an average of £755 each on their hobby every year. It's difficult to cut that cost without giving up altogether – and keeping up our pastimes and pleasures is essential for general happiness and wellbeing. But whatever your chosen activity, you could cut costs by clubbing together with others.

- **Sharing equipment**: This could save you spending hundreds of pounds on the necessary golf clubs or tennis rackets.

- **Sharing travelling expenses**: Do this by driving together to your club or venue, and it will obviously save money on petrol.

- **Safety in numbers**: If you have to hire a court, the more of you playing, the cheaper it will be. If you're a tennis player, for instance, playing doubles rather than singles will halve the cost of the court for you and, frankly, can be a lot more fun.

- **Share cost**: It may even be possible to share the cost of club membership.

Be Ruthless

If you do have lots of sports equipment, decide whether you really need it. Selling off an old set of golf clubs or other equipment on eBay or Gumtree could net you a decent cash bonus.

Look Out for Deals

It's also worth keeping your eyes peeled for cut-price offers. Golfers can cut the cost of a round by making use of two-for-one offers across 950 courses, for instance. You'll find details of the vouchers – which cost £2.50 – at www.todaysgolfer.co.uk.

Leisure

It is essential for your peace of mind and general welfare to relax and have fun as part of your daily routine. But you don't need to spend a fortune to enjoy yourself. Just watch children playing for proof of that. Buy them an expensive toy, and many will have more fun playing with the box it came in. For adults it's a little different. The joys of playing with a cardboard box soon become limited. But you can take part in or watch sport relatively cheaply. There are bargain cinema and theatre tickets to be had, and books and music can be enjoyed for free.

Going Out

However you like to enjoy yourself when going out, there are ways to have a great evening – or afternoon – without breaking the bank.

Watch Cheaper Football

Tickets for Premiership football matches have never been more expensive. If you are keen enough to get a season ticket, split the costs with friends. If the team is popular enough, there should a queue of people willing to take match tickets off your hands – even for those wet midweek evening games that you don't usually bother going to.

 Lower division: Even better – don't pay Premiership prices to watch live football. Instead look around for a local side in a lower division. The football may not be world class, but the entertainment value will be high, and you may be surprised at how pleasant the crowd is compared to some of the more vociferous fans you find at Premier League grounds. At Chelsea in the current 2008–09 season, for instance, you'll be charged around £50 to see a Premier League match. Head down the road to AFC Wimbledon, who play in the Blue Square South League, and entrance is just £10 and, some believe, a whole lot more fun.

Kids: If you have kids to take to games, the savings are even more stark. Children's tickets at Chelsea and other leading clubs sell out almost instantly, so most parents are forced to stump up an extra £50 or so for every child they take to a game. At Wimbledon in the 2008–09 season, terrace tickets for kids are just £2. In other words, they could see 25 games – more than a whole season of home matches – for the price of one match in the top flight.

Cinema – Off-Peak and Deals

Friday or Saturday nights are peak times for cinemas, and that's when prices are highest. But go when the cinemas are traditionally empty, and you can see the latest films – or fairly recent ones – at a fraction of the cost.

Discounts: Many cinemas offer family films at just £1 a head on a Saturday morning, for instance. That's £1 for adults as well as kids. Which means a family of four can see a movie at the pictures for just £4, rather than the £20 or more that it usually costs. Other cinemas do cut-price pensioner specials on Tuesdays when, again, you can see recent movies for much less than the normal price.

Orange Wednesdays: There are also offers you could take advantage of. On Wednesdays, for instance, subscribers to the Orange mobile phone network can get a 2for1 entry code for certain cinemas just by making a call or sending a text to 241. Take a friend, and you're both effectively paying half-price for the latest movie.

Pay Less For the Theatre

West End theatre prices are very high, with stalls costing £60 at leading shows. If you're a fan of the theatre, what are your options?

Seats: Choose seats further away. Up in the gods, for instance, prices can be a third of the cost of front-row seats.

Discount booth: Visit the half-price ticket booth in London's Leicester Square. They may not have the exact show you want to see at a bargain price, but they always have a decent selection of plays and musicals – often including some of the current hot tickets – which should satisfy most theatre fans. Tickets aren't exactly half-price because the booth adds on a booking fee, but they are considerably cheaper than standard-price tickets.

Online: Get cut-price tickets for West End shows online. For instance, www.lastminute.com always has a selection of cheap deals from as little as £10. Many include dinner at a restaurant local to the theatre to save even more money.

Local theatre: If a trip to the West End is just a little too expensive, check out the attractions at your local theatre. Many West End productions do a post-London tour of the country, allowing you to see the stars and the critically acclaimed shows in your home town for much less money – and no expensive travel costs to London.

Eating Out

Many restaurant chains have regular discount deals, and taking advantage of them will mean a family meal, for instance, becomes a little more affordable. Two-for-one promotions are regularly run in newspapers, and it's worth spending the 40–80p on a paper if you end up saving £10 or more on a meal. There are also regular meal deals offered. You can track down

vouchers and offers online at sites such as www.hotukdeals.com or www.myvouchercodes.co.uk. Other sites such as www.lastminute.com often have exclusive offers with certain restaurants and their theatre-meal deals can save you a packet.

Be on TV

With so many reality programmes and quiz shows on TV these days, there's every chance of getting on the small screen yourself. If you'd like to be in the audience for a show, you can register for tickets at www.applausestore.com. The company sorts out the audience for shows such as *Big Brother* and *Dancing on Ice*, so you could be in for a great free night out. If there's a BBC show you'd like to participate in, then go to shows.external.bbc.co.uk. There you'll find details of upcoming availability for audience members for all BBC shows, whether TV or radio.

Or maybe you would like to do more than just be in the audience? Pick the right show, and you could end up being quids in too. If you enjoy watching quiz shows, for instance, and often find yourself shouting out the answers at the telly, imagine how much more fun it would be to be on one. All shows need contestants, so why shouldn't it be you? And if you get on, you won't just have a great time – you'll also be in with a chance of getting a great prize. Check on www.iqagb.co.uk – the 'largest quizzing website' in the UK – for details of shows looking for contestants. It includes application forms for classic shows such as *Countdown*, as well as details of how to apply for new and upcoming quiz shows.

Staying In

There are lots of free ways to amuse yourself and family and friends at home, whether it's old games or new ones. You can also cut down on the considerable cost of watching telly.

Scrap the Subscription

Satellite and cable television subscriptions can top £500 a year. That's a lot of cash – especially when you can now get digital TV – with a choice of up to 80 channels – for free. Freeview and

Freesat both offer a range of entertainment and children's channels, and plenty of other channels that you'll want to watch. Giving up the 100s offered by Sky or Virgin may be hard, but you will still have plenty of choice. Most new televisions now come complete with a Freeview tuner, so you won't even have to pay the £50 or so for that.

DVDs

If you like watching films, hiring DVDs from your local library when you need them will work out a lot cheaper than paying the monthly cost of a film channel. Or you could look out for free trial periods from DVD film clubs, such as Lovefilm. Take up the offer, then cancel before the period ends, to see the latest DVDs for free. You'll be able to do this only once, mind!

Watch TV on Your Computer

If you're thinking of getting a second TV for the bedroom or kitchen, don't. Instead watch shows on your computer or laptop. Once BBC television programmes have been broadcast, you can watch them on your computer using the BBC iPlayer, for instance. You can even plug your computer into your TV if you want to watch the shows on the big screen.

Read for Free

Heard of libraries? They're absolutely great for free reading material, not just books. Books are their main thing, of course, and you can order anything you like – including all the latest bestsellers or nonfiction books you might need. There may be a waiting list for really popular books, but order early and you won't have to wait long. But it's not only books that are on hand.

Papers and mags: Most libraries have the daily papers available for you to look at, as well as a selection of magazines. You can't take them home, but you can save on expensive subscriptions by catching up with your monthly magazine there. Take consumer magazine *Which?*, for instance. It's a good example because it's full of tips to save you money, and you could save the £78 annual subscription by reading issues at your library.

 Swapping: Another way to get free books is through the Read It-Swap It scheme. Simply register as a member at www.readitswapit.co.uk, and you'll get access to almost 200,000 different books. It works on a simple swap basis. You search for the book you want, then contact the person who has it. They then send you the book and you read it, before offering it back on the site. The only cost is postage, and there's a feedback system to ensure people don't abuse the system and simply collect books or not send the books they've promised to. There is a cost when you start sending books. Postage can be around £1.40, depending on the weight or size of the book. But it's still considerably cheaper than buying it.

Play Games

When was the last time you took a board game out of the cupboard? Games such as Cluedo, Jenga and Trivial Pursuit can be great fun and make for a free evening's entertainment. Invite friends or family over to increase the enjoyment. Get everyone to bring their own food and drink, and the cost will be low for all. It doesn't have to be a board game. You could play cards or one of the great traditional parlour games, such as consequences, charades or who's in the hat.

Cutting Down

Reducing the amount of money you spend on drink or cigarettes could be the best thing you ever did. Not only will you save cash, but you'll also help your health improve. Think about how much you spend on expensive coffees too.

Smoking

Aside from the obvious health issues, there are instant financial benefits to giving up smoking. In the first month you could be better off by around £170 if you give up a 20-a-day habit. Over a year that tots up to £2,040 – which could go a long way towards helping you to cope with other bills.

Higher savings: In fact the average smoker is predicted to smoke 30 cigarettes per day. Based on a cost of £5.50 per packet for 20 cigarettes, if a smoker kicked their habit, they could save £250 per month. That adds up to £3,000 a year, which means that over 10 years you'd end up with more than £30,000 extra in your pocket by giving up smoking.

Health: There are also the massive health benefits, of course. Stopping smoking reduces your risk of lung cancer, heart attacks and strokes. In fact your health starts to improve within minutes. Within ten years of stopping, your chances of having a heart attack have fallen to the same as someone who's never smoked.

Insurance: Giving up smoking will also have other financial benefits. The cost of life insurance could be halved, for instance. For example, a 35-year-old male smoker taking out a £100,000 policy over 25 years would be charged around £20 a month for premiums. A nonsmoker would be charged only around £10. Over the term of the policy that means the nonsmoker would save more than £3,000. You won't get cheaper premiums right away, but most life assurance companies consider customers to be nonsmokers if they have not smoked for 12 months.

Get help: There's a free smoking helpline from the NHS on 0800 022 4332. Or go online to the NHS website gosmokefree.nhs.uk for advice and help. You can also get free professional advice on quitting smoking at www.bupa.co.uk/health.

Drinking

Cutting back on the amount you drink will save cash and improve your health. Think about how much alcohol you drink every week. Do you finish a couple of bottles of wine a week? Or sink a few pints after work? It all adds up. Two bottles of wine a week at, say, a fiver each, works out at more than £500 a year. Ten pints of beer a week could be costing you more than £1,000 a year depending on which part of the country you live. In London it would set you back nearer to £1,500 over the course of a year.

 Change brands: Cutting down will clearly help your family budget. But you could also save more by buying cheaper brands. If you're having guests over, for instance, buying cheaper wine and pouring it into a decanter will almost certainly fool most guests, unless you've bought a particularly poor bottle. The same is true of spirits. No one will notice a bargain bottle of vodka or gin if it's been decanted first, then served with a mixer.

✓ **Water:** You can and should also save on bottled water. Refill bottles from a tap. No one can really tell the difference. In a recent test even experts were fooled, with many choosing tap water as the best-tasting. The fact is, Britain has among the cleanest tap water in the world, and it is perfectly safe to drink. Put it in the fridge to chill before drinking, and you really won't notice the difference.

✓ **Brew your own:** If you like drinking beer at home, get a brew-your-own kit. These days they won't blow up in the airing cupboard or under the stairs. They make perfectly palatable ale and lager – and for as little as 15p a pint.

Say No to Cappuccino

If you've got an expensive coffee habit, it's time to give it up. Drink tap water instead. It's free and, unlike coffee, doesn't stain your teeth or damage your waistline. By cutting out your daily cappuccino with full-fat milk, you could save around £50 a month. That soon mounts up to £600 a year. There are health benefits too. Giving up full-fat coffee for a month will mean cutting back on 3,652 calories. And saying goodbye to caffeine can also help you to get a good night's sleep. You'll end up with a healthier body and mind, as well as being wealthier.

Entertaining Children

Kids have great imagination and can be easily entertained without spending any money. Sometimes you just need to help them along in their imaginary games.

Libraries

Libraries are great places for kids. Not only do they provide free books or audio stories, but also they often hold reading sessions and other activities aimed at children. Get your children into the habit of visiting the library every week, and they'll thank you in years to come.

Packaging

Old packaging can be the kick-start to a world of adventure. A big cardboard box – one that may have contained a television or cooker, for instance – can quickly become a pirate's galleon, Dr Who's Tardis or a secret club hiding place. If you use your imagination, you will help children to use theirs.

Dressing Up

Old clothes are great for dressing-up games, which most kids love. They can become whatever character they like and may even want to take it further and put on a show for you. Encourage them to do so and help them with the script, and they could be quietly entertained for hours. And at no cost!

Cinema

If they love the cinema, take them to £1-a-head Saturday morning showings.

Little Ones

If you have children under the age of six, join the Early Learning Centre's Big Birthday Club. It's free to join, and you will receive a 20 per cent voucher a month before your child's birthday. It's also worth registering with Mothercare to get details of exclusive offers and discounts throughout the year.

Clothes and Appearance

Clothes shopping is fun – but expensive. Finding ways to refresh your outfits cheaply or make clothes go further are essential when you're watching your pennies. Don't forget to check out the Shopping section (pages 62–97) for further details.

Keep it Simple

For starters, don't buy lots of fashionable new clothes. Instead buy a cheap, plain work outfit which you can easily dress up with a bit of colour to go out at night. You'll be able to wear the right outfit in different ways every day with a little bit of mix 'n' match.

Maintenance and Customization

Instead of throwing out damaged clothing, repair it. If a shirt has a broken or missing button, simply sew on a new one. Get the sewing kit out to bring your wardrobe up to date. Put some military-looking buttons on an old jacket, for instance, to get a fashionable army-style coat. Take in or turn up last season's trousers to bring them bang up to style. If you have old faded jeans, get some black dye and turn them into a snappy Goth look.

Charity Shops

If you've always turned your nose up at charity shops for clothes, think again. Oxfam is opening a number of boutique-style shops with designer second-hand clothes. All the fashion at a fraction of the price.

Swap Shops

How about swapping your unwanted clothes? It's the latest Internet trend, where people swap fashion mistakes for something of a similar value. Go to www.whatsmineisyours.com or www.bigwardrobe.com to start swapping.

Get Cut-Price Haircuts

You may need to be feeling brave, but you can get bargain hair cuts or highlights by agreeing to have your hair done by a trainee hairdresser.

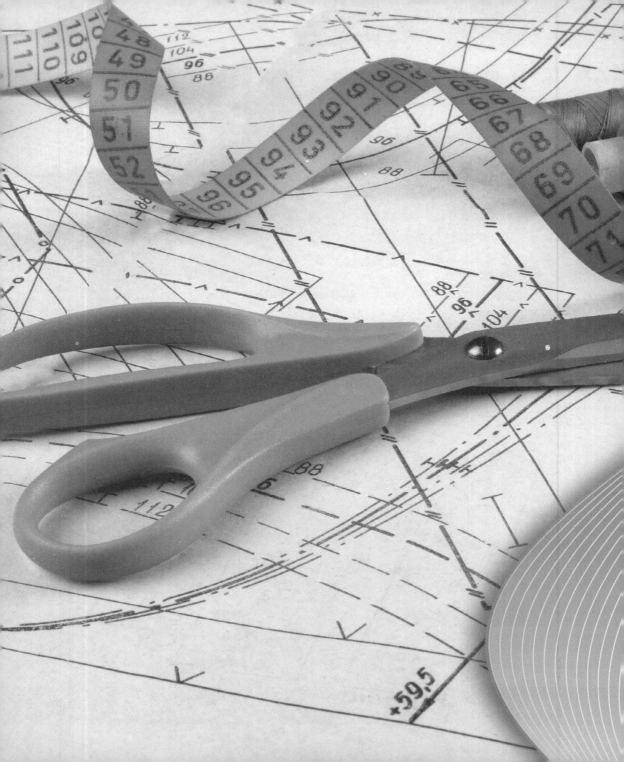

Making Money from Home

Selling What You Have

Whether you are stay-at-home mum with a couple of hours to kill while the kids are at school or a full-time employee with a nightly passion for eBay, there are ways you can beat the credit crunch by earning from the comfort of your own pad. From de-cluttering for cash or making the most out of your home, you can earn extra money without leaving your home.

Selling Your Wares From Home

The recent credit crunch is quite different from the downturn in the 1970s, as these days many of us are sitting on a houseful of clutter we have gathered over the past few decades of consumerism. But this can be turned into pounds and pence via a number of channels. And once it is sold, you will find that not only is your wallet heavier, but your home and conscience are lighter too.

Flog the Garage Clutter on eBay

These days auction website www.eBay.com (or www.eBay.co.uk if you're buying in the UK) has become something of an institution. In theory, you can sell anything on the site from fish tanks to fertilizer by listing the item, sitting back and watching people bid to buy it – all from the comfort of your living room. Bear in mind, though, that there are charges involved. For example, if you sell an item for £5 and charge £2 for packing and posting, you will pay an approximate 51p fee to eBay – but given the fact you are making something out of what is effectively nothing, the situation is a win-win.

Sell the Kids' Old Bikes Through the Local Rag

Bulkier items, such as kids' old bikes and scooters, might prove too much hassle and expense to sell to parents that live on the other side of the country. But don't let them clog up your

garage either. Instead, support your local newspaper by placing an advert in its classified section, stating that the item must be collected. Even if you make a £5 profit once you have paid for the advert, it's been no effort to you, a bargain to the buyer and it will feel good to give an old bike a new lease of life.

Set Up a Stall Outside

While this is no good if you live in a cul-de-sac, if you have a house with a driveway on a busy street – especially if it sees a high number of pedestrians – why not set up a stall outside selling unwanted bric-a-brac such as books, CDs and clean clothes in good condition? To make things simple, you could put a set price on each item, say, 50p or £1.

Dig Out Family Heirlooms

If you have lived in your home for some time, there is no telling what you might find in the loft – especially if you are storing belongings from grandparents that have since passed away. If you find an unusual relic that's been passed down through the family, send a picture of it to the British Antique Dealers' Association (BADA) at www.bada.org. If it is found to be of any value, BADA will pass on the details to an antique dealer who may want to buy it.

Get Commercial With Your Bricks and Mortar

As much as we love our homes, most of the time they are taking a good chunk of our hard-earned cash, whether it's in mortgage costs, energy bills, council tax or just maintenance and repairs. So when things get tough, why not make your bricks and mortar work a little for their own keep? Try the following.

Rent Out Unwanted Space

You can make an average of £289 per month from renting out a spare room, according to research from Abbey, which is the kind of money that could make a real difference to your income. This is especially the case if you are one of the 1.8 million people that the Council of Mortgage Lenders estimates will be facing a mortgage payment shock this year. And you can receive up to £4,250 tax-free gross rental income a year under the government's Rent-a Room scheme.

Go Into Bed and Breakfast

If you live in one of the UK's hot tourist spots, why not look at providing a bed-and-breakfast service? This would tie in well with the growing trend of families deciding to stay in the UK for their annual breaks. You will need to research the bed and breakfast market thoroughly, though, and where you stand legally. As you will be changing the terms of your property, you may need planning permission and to review your insurance. Take a course in opening a B&B at www.bedandbreakfastacademy.co.uk.

Use Your Property for a Film Location

Film and TV companies always require a wide range of properties when they are on location, so register yours. You don't need a country mansion to qualify – companies are on the lookout for everything from cottages to council flats. As well as earning up to £20,000 extra in a year, if your home features in a blockbuster movie, this could even increase its value. You can register your home at www.mylocations.co.uk.

Offer Your Drive as a Parking Space

If you live in a busy city near public transport such as the tube or close to the station in a commuter town, your driveway is hot property. Renting it out can make you up to £400 a month, which – if you don't have a car at all – is madness to turn down. You can register your driveway at www.parkatmyhouse.com.

Offer Your Garage as Storage Space

With space at a premium, a garage is a luxury in some parts of the UK. So if yours is lying fallow, why not rent it out as storage? This might be a long-term arrangement for someone who has moved abroad for a few years, or just for a few days if someone has sold their home and is waiting to move into the next one. If you live near a local organization – such as a boat club or even running club that needs storage for giant clocks at races – you could approach them too.

Sell Some of Your Land

Despite house-price falls, land on our tiny island is still priced at a huge premium. If there is building work going on around you, offer to sell the developers a strip of your garden. If it translates into a garage or separate driveway for the property that's being built, the developer could be biting your hand off, leaving you thousands of pounds better off. But make sure that you factor into the deal which party is going to pay for the legal fees.

Selling What You Can Do

It's usually much easier to save than to earn and, in times of a credit crunch, that is the order of preference that people usually take. However, the advent of domestic technology and a working culture that is increasingly centred on the home has resulted in more opportunity for struggling consumers to generate cash from extra work at home. So whether it's giving language or music lessons, or looking after someone's dog, there is definitely money out there to be made by utilizing your skills and capabilities.

Selling Your Time and Skills From Home

We all have skills and talents, but they are often left on the back burner as work or family commitments take daily priority. But turn the credit crunch to your creative favour by revisiting these skills and turning them into money-making opportunities that you can carry out from home. You might surprise yourself.

Learn to Build a Website

It might sound insurmountable at first, but learning to build websites is perfectly straightforward and achievable. And when you know what you are doing, you can offer your web-building services to local businesses that perhaps have yet to establish that crucial online presence. This is a perfect job for a stay-at-home mum. who can go between computer and baby at the drop of a hat. Kick off your learning curve with a course such as www.buildwebsite4u.com.

Give Music Lessons

If you spent years of your life being marched to piano lessons, put the experience to good use in adulthood by advertising your services in the local newspaper as a music teacher. If your level of confidence gets the better of you, just specify that you tutor only beginners or cap your teaching at a certain grade. Just three hour-long lessons as week could see you up to £60 better off, not to mention the sense of satisfaction you will get. The same applies for languages.

Tutor a Child

If you gave up a teaching job to start a family or even recently retired as a teacher, why let your knowledge, experience and expertise go to waste? One-to-one tutoring from someone who is both familiar and respected is always snapped up by parents, which means that you can earn some pocket money and still achieve job fulfilment – but in your own time and on your own terms.

Arrange Flowers

The stereotype of the elderly ladies at church arranging flowers over a cup of tea and a biscuit is long gone. These days an artistic and competent flower arranger can earn serious bucks.

For example, according to research from Alliance & Leicester, couples about to tie the knot budget for an average £550 on flowers for their big day. Get a chunk of this cash by setting up as a freelance flower arranger.

Make Wedding Cakes

Average weddings costs a staggering £19,400 according to wedding website www.confetti.co.uk, indicating how much couples are prepared to spend on getting details such as the cake absolutely perfect. However, like anyone else, brides and grooms are suffering from the effects of the credit crunch. So if baking comes as second nature, why not try some of your own designs and undercut the big wedding cake suppliers? As a benchmark, £250 is a rock-bottom price.

Be a Seamstress

The generation that can sew would be flabbergasted to learn how much money people spend on having the hem of a skirt taken down or different buttons sewn onto a shirt. This is because

they know it takes five minutes and costs pence. If you are part of this generation or a simply creative and entrepreneurial, why not turn these skills into cash?

Become a Beautician

When it comes to haircuts, manicures and leg waxing, women can be very particular about who they go to. If you studied beauty and know you are good at these treatments and others, why not set up at home? Once you have a satisfied stream of customers, they are very likely to return – especially if you undercut the big expensive spa chains and hairdressers in town.

Get Typing

When you have been able to touch type for years, it can be hard to believe how long some people take in just getting their ideas down on an electronic page. Sign up with a secretarial agency and specify that you are looking for typing work at home – or advertise in local schools and universities that may need dissertations or letters typed.

Start a Dog-Washing Service

Keeping a dog fit, well and healthy is not cheap, so pet owners may be looking for ways to cut costs in the credit crunch. Tap into this market by setting up your own dog-washing business. You'll need a garage and a strong resilience to mess – but you'll earn money without having to leave the house.

Send an Article to a Newspaper

Did well in English and fancy your chances as a writer? Thanks to the Internet, this money-making opportunity is more real than ever. Look carefully at the style of your chosen magazine or section of a newspaper, and write a topical article. Then send it by email to the editor with a clear heading in the subject bar. If it's published, you could make an immediate £200 or more – and have your name in print.

Do Ironing for the Time-Poor

For people in a full-time job and juggling family commitments, ironing gets pushed to the very bottom of the priority list. But it doesn't go away either – and therein lies the problem. If you have a few hours to spare, advertise your ironing services to local commuters.

Get into Telesales

You don't need to be in a call centre to sell successfully over the phone. Sign up to a recruitment agency that deals in telesales from home where, without the pressure, you will probably achieve better results anyway.

Sign Up With AQA

Text question-and-answer service AQA – which stands for Any Question Answered – is always looking for people who can supply answers to a constant supply of questions that are sent via mobile phones. These could be related to absolutely anything from directions to abstract thoughts such as 'What would actually happen if we blamed it on the boogie?' (The answer to this one incidentally was: 'If we did blame it on the boogie, the boogie would desert the human race, leaving us genuinely unable to control our feet.') You can have a lot of fun and earn money every time you choose to answer.

Trade on the Stock Markets Online

The credit crunch may have seen the price of shares plummet, but it's also an interesting time for investors looking to buy at the bottom of the market. But whenever you think that could be, at least being at home and on the PC is a great place to monitor the price of shares. However, you will need to do your homework thoroughly before getting into online share-dealing – and keep in mind that investments, just like property prices, can go down as well as up.

Enter Competitions

At one time you could enter competitions for just the price of a stamp, but nowadays it's free online. The more you enter, the greater chance you have of winning. And even if the prize is a voucher for a theme park, it all saves money. It's probably a good idea to set up a separate email account, though, so you are not inundated with spam.

Negotiate With Your Boss

While you may first have to prove your worth with your employer for a couple of years, many PAYE jobs can be carried out from home the same as from an office. See if you can negotiate a couple of days in the week when you can do your existing job from home. This would save on travel, stress and even the cost of lunch. But be sure to tell your boss the bonuses are not just on your side – without travel you are likely to start earlier and finish later – and happy, relaxed staff are infinitely more productive.

Cash in on Comfort

As well as the bricks and mortar of your home pulling their weight, you can generate some cash through commercial hospitality too. Consider the following.

Host an Ann Summers Party

Send the boys to the pub, and host an Ann Summers party in your front room. Not only is this a lot of fun and the perfect excuse for a girl's get together, but you can make some considerable cash too. And to top it all off, your friends will not be spending any more than they would on a night out on the town. You can apply to become an Ann Summers party organizer at www.annsummers.com.

Start a Babysitting Service for Friends

Every parent wants their child to be left in the hands of someone they know and trust, while, for a child, staying the night at family friend's house is fun. If you need to earn some extra cash and your friends need a weekend away without the kids, combine the two needs for an outcome that suits three parties.

Look After People's Animals

Pet owner's holidays can often be tarnished through worry about leaving a pet in a cattery or kennel – or even on their own at home for a fortnight. Set up as an in-house Dr Doolittle by taking in loved animals and making sure they are still loved while their family is away on holiday.

Gifts

Make Your Own

Celebrations – and the gifts we give to acknowledge them – do not have to break the bank. There are plenty of money-saving (and thought-generous) gift ideas to be had. We'll start with gifts that come from your own dear hands – time, effort and thought are all qualities that mean so much more than money. And having spent decades battling through a maze of consumerism, people become immediately excited about the prospect of owning an item that's so 'limited edition'. A bit of DIY can go a long way when it comes to giving gifts.

Art and Needlework

Make Your Own Cards

A personalized card is certain to put a smile on anyone's face. All you need is an old picture of them that they didn't know you had and an appropriate speech bubble. If you want to get more creative, why not buy a packet of blank cards and some materials and decorations from an arts and crafts shop? Another alternative is to use an online personalized card service, such as www.greetz.co.uk, where you can get the first card free and further discounts if you continue to use the site.

Write a Poem or Story

Creativity takes all sorts of forms, and it may be that yours is with a pen and paper. A funny poem on a birthday is always well received, and, if you write a story for a small child, you can even have it bound professionally. Visit www.signaturebindings.co.uk for more details.

Knitting

Once thought of as a pastime for chattering old ladies, knitting has made a real comeback in recent years. Knitting clubs and networks, where you can make friends while stocking up on kitsch and unusual presents for your loved ones to give during the year, are springing up all over the country. You can make gifts for newborn babies or even personalized clothes for children's dolls. Look at www.castoff.info for information on how to get started.

Sewing

Cross-stitch is easy, but the effect can look very impressive. Pick out a set featuring an interest of the recipient, such as a dog or cat. You can also stitch the name of a newborn child and put it in a frame for the nursery wall or make a tablecloth for a parent or grandparent. Cross-stitch sets can be bought quite cheaply at any arts and crafts shop, or you can buy one online at www.readicut.co.uk

Kitchen and Garden Produce

Home Horticulture

It seems easy to drop into a petrol station and pick up a bunch of flowers. But a closer look at the price, as well as quality of the bunch, is likely to be enough to make you want to grow your own. A single rose from your garden wrapped in brown paper is far more memorable, or even a potted plant courtesy of your own soil — just make sure the recipient knows that it's a product of home horticulture.

Give a Home-Grown Takeaway

Ever received a home-made vegetable curry or stew as a present? I am sure the answer is no, but wouldn't it be great? Especially if the vegetables were cultivated in your friend's garden. Growing everything from carrots to potatoes in a vegetable patch or allotment, and turning them into a friend's favourite dish that can be frozen and packaged up as a present is a really quirky, thoughtful way to say happy birthday. Get started at www.realseeds.co.uk.

Make Some Cakes

A home-made sponge, apple or fruit cake can make a great novelty present and double up as a birthday cake if you stick some candles in the top. Even a box of chocolate cookies or flapjacks would be equally well received – and you may find that you have most if the ingredients already in the cupboard.

Personalized Gifts

Frame a Photograph

Make your home computer start to pay its way. Track down some old photographs of your friend (perhaps from school days or when you first met), scan them into the computer and print off. Your only investment then is a photograph frame – you may even have one you can use – and, hey presto, a thoughtful gift comprised of existing resources that you know will never end up consigned to the bin.

Bring the Past to the Present

Revamping an old black-and-white picture of grandparents or even great-grandparents and turning it into a framed present is a great idea. Especially because at the same time you can make sure that these precious memories are not lost or spoiled beyond recognition with time.

Make a Small Album or Picture CD

If you can find a few pictures, put them in small album instead, or download as many as you like onto a CD, which can also be sent easily through the post.

Make a DVD

Wedding presents can be the most expensive of all, but modern couples are often already kitted out with furniture and kitchenware. All the more reason then to ask one of your more technical friends to record a DVD featuring a bunch of you talking to camera about funny memories and leaving wishes for the future.

Restore an Old Relic

If your loved one had a special belonging that has been forgotten with time, why not give it the kiss of life? For example, stitching a missing eye onto a teddy bear or putting a new stylus in an old record player and digging out the vinyl. All this costs is a little time and patience, and perhaps a birthday bow for good measure.

Research Your Family Tree

While you will certainly need some time for this one, you won't need any cash. Tracing back your ancestors and packaging up your findings could be the best present a family member has ever received in their life. Visit www.genesreunited.co.uk for an initial springboard.

Use What You Have

If you look at the bottom of your cupboards, you are more than likely to find treasures that have long been forgotten. Make sure that you dig them out and use them again before hitting the shops for more.

Create an Event

All children really ever need is to feel special – and this doesn't have to cost money. They are more likely to remember events than objects. Same goes for most adults too!

Use Cost-Free Fresh Air

Memories of a birthday picnic in the park with sandwiches, drinks and a few games are the kind that last a lifetime, and it need only cost a few pounds. Smaller children may enjoy a trip to the farm or animal sanctuary, which just requires a small donation rather than forking out an entry fee for each toddler.

Utilize the Home You Already Pay For

If it's raining or a child's birthday falls in the winter, you still don't have to foot the expense of a meal out for 30. Gather as much adult support together as you can, and host a party at home. Traditional games such as musical bumps, musical chairs, pass the parcel and sleeping lions go down a treat, while treasure hunts around the house with a prize at the end are fun too. For more ideas, invest a few pounds in Jane Kemp's *Party Games* guide from her Practical Parents series, which is available on Amazon.

Hire Party CDs From Your Local Library

You don't need to buy party CDs for children's parties or festive celebrations. Have a browse in your local library and see what you can borrow for nothing.

Revisit the Dinner Party

You won't be the only one in your circle of friends who will be feeling the credit crunch, so why not turn your back on expensive meals out and take a trip back to the 1970s dinner party? You could each take a turn in hosting and even embrace the retro feel by serving up cheese and pineapple sticks or Viennetta ice cream for desert.

Recycle Wrapping Paper

Pretty as it may be, just one thick sheet of wrapping paper can cost more than £2 these days, and if you want a decoration to go with it you can double that price. But it's extras such as this that can suddenly hike up costs. In this case, reuse old wrapping paper, tucking under tears and blemishes. Bags for wine bottles are especially easy to reuse – and especially wasteful to throw away.

Shop and Celebrate Sensibly

When you do have to go to the shops to buy presents, or are having a celebration in a restaurant, make sure you don't buy into the marketing too. Start out in control of your spending, and don't let the commercial machine shake your resolve.

Shopping

Use Discount Vouchers For Presents

These days, there are a whole host web-based discount vouchers available with which you can buy exactly the same gift – simply for less money. Look at sites such as www.codes.co.uk that carries 34,000 vouchers you can use at 1,200 retailers.

Shop For the Same Present For Less

If you want to buy, say, a DVD or CD for someone's birthday, a record store on the high street such as HMV would have been your first port of call a few years back. However, when there is absolutely no difference in the product, you may pay a premium for the name. Woolworths is often a much cheaper stockist of DVDs and CDs, while if you go online to www.play.com it will be cheaper still. And if you buy two gifts simultaneously, you may qualify for free delivery.

Get Presents For Free

If you know that your loved one has been looking for something specific or unusual that went out of production some years ago, you might find it on www.freecycle.co.uk.

This is an excellent online resource of local residents in your area that are giving away things. There are two rules – the first is that no money must change hands, and the second is that you must have started giving to receive.

Buy Your Christmas Paper in January
The cost of posh wrapping paper and decorations plummets like a stone in January. But when the rest of the nation is all 'Christmassed out' is the most economic time to stock up.

Use Loyalty Cards
Christmas is the time to bring out all the loyalty cards you have been saving points on during the course of the year. Even if you have just been collecting points at your supermarket, remember that they can be used for a whole range of gifts, such as CDs, books, perfume, clothes and homeware – in addition to the staple Christmas meal shop.

Don't Fall Foul of Retailers' Tricks
Mother's Day is a prime example of when pre-packaged, cleverly placed flowers and chocolates suddenly seem to double in price. Avoid the draw of the display and temptation of convenience, and seek out your own flowers.

Use the Sales
While you may not feel like shopping for winter clothes as spring approaches, or for hats and flip flops as it starts to turn nippy outside, this approach to shopping for gifts can save you a fortune. Simply store them in the bottom of your wardrobe, and bring them out as presents the next time the season is right.

Buy Second-Hand

Vintage clothes, coats and bags don't all have to be bought from trendy shops that charge more for the item than it would cost new. If you have an eye for fashion, scour the local second-hand shops. They are unlikely to be able to tell the difference between vintage and just old – and will charge accordingly. Give the item a wash, and package it up into an original birthday or Christmas present.

Don't Forget Postage

Having a present wrapped and sitting on your sideboard is only part of the equation. If you have to post the item – especially recorded delivery – you will need to factor this into your budget in advance. But if you have opted to buy online, why not send it straight to the address of your friend? Make up for the plain packing with a follow-up phone call.

Make a Lucky Dip

No one said a birthday present had to have any value. It's much more important that it is fun and tailored to its recipient's personality. In this case, you could make a lucky dip containing funny items or memories, such as their favourite chocolate bar or lottery ticket.

Celebrations

Celebrations may be expected in addition to presents, so it is imperative to keep the costs down.

Cater For People Cheaply

When you are the main supplier of the party food, don't panic about the bill. A big bowl full of oven-baked jacket potatoes and an array of different fillings, ranging from cheese to tuna, will keep everyone happy without breaking the bank. And it's more than likely someone will offer to bring dessert or some bottles of wine anyway.

Use Vouchers For Birthday Cinema Outings

If you opt for a treat to the cinema, paying full price for each child will soon add up. But, as well as Orange Wednesdays, which offer two for one every Wednesday by texting from an Orange phone, the three large multiplex chains – Vue, Odeon and Cineworld – all offer cheap weekend deals for families.

Don't Pay Full Price For Birthday Meals

If you are having a birthday meal out, make sure that you use a restaurant that is running a promotional discount. These have been very popular since consumers stated to rein in their spending, as restaurants try any trick they can to win back customers. Vouchers can be found in newspapers or downloaded from the Internet at www.vouchercodes.com.

Book a Restaurant in Advance Online

If you are planning an evening out at a special restaurant, how the reservation was made will make no difference to the experience or the food, but it may leave you feeling financially lighter. Book far enough in advance at www.toptable.co.uk, and get up to 50 per cent off the bill.

Make a Pact to Spend Less

A key point to remember in every credit crunch is that everyone else will be feeling it too. This means that cost-saving ideas when it comes to gifts and celebrations are likely to be met with open arms. So start the ball rolling with the following and wait for the result.

Agree Present Price Limits in Advance

The suggestion that people put a blanket cap on present prices, especially at Christmas, will probably be met with a surge of relief. While, on first thought, you may wonder what you can buy for £5 or £10 a head, that's all part of the fun. The more limited your financial resource, the harder you will have to think.

Chip in With a Group

Having a group of people all put in less than they would individually for a gift – whether it's for a birthday, wedding or anniversary – still means that the final pot is bigger. And, as the credit crunch makes it less likely that recipients will buy major items or experiences – such as a spa treatment – for themselves, being able to do it for them keeps everybody happy.

Be Honest

Remembering and acknowledging an occasion has always carried more weight than sending something that's expensive but late and without thought. If you are struggling to make ends meet this year, simply explain the situation and give something that's virtually free such as a phone call or letter. And if you are chipping in among good friends, remember that the contributions don't have to be equal – they just need to reflect that you are all thinking about the recipient. If you feel uncomfortable about putting in less, opt to give your time instead by organizing and wrapping the gift.

Agree Not to Buy For Adults

Times have changed since the last economic downturn of the 1970s when a new serving dish or LP would have sent hearts racing. Now it seems people have all the material things they need, in which case it seems futile to continue to pump money into the commercial machine. When it comes to Christmas, why not agree that you will just buy presents for children, which will save all the adults a fortune?

Remember What a Stocking is For

Whether Father Christmas has been hit by the credit crunch or not, the stocking full of presents he leaves behind on Christmas Eve may have to be. But the fun of a stocking is opening lots of individual packets more than really wanting what's inside them. Keep things fun and cheap – and don't forget the best bit was always the satsuma anyway.

Further Reading

Bamford, M., *The Money Tree*, Prentice Hall, 2006

Bredenberg, J., *Amazing Insider Secrets: 1703 Money-Saving Tips*, Reader's Digest Association, 2008

Briggs, M., *Bicarbonate of Soda: A Very Versatile Natural Substance*, Black and White Publishing, 2007

Briggs, M., *Green Cleaning: Natural Hints and Tips*, Abbeydale Press, 2008

Callaghan, G., Fribbance, I. and Higginson, M., *Personal Finance*, John Wiley & Sons, 2006

Costantino, M. and Steer, G., *Vinegar: All You Need for Everyday Use*, Star Fire, 2007

Delquadro, K., *Making Great Bags, Tags, Boxes and Cards*, Sterling, 2006

Doncaster, L., *150 Low Budget Recipes for Delicious Meals Every Day*, South Water, 2008

Evans, H., *Making Money from Your Home*, Piatkus Books, 1994

Faulkner, K., *Renting and Letting*, Which? Books, 2008

Furnival, J., *Smart Saving*, Hay House Inc, 2007

Gilruth, G., *Making Mini Cards, Gift Tags and Invitations*, Guild of Master Craftsman Publications Ltd, 2000

Ides, N.L., *Hand Mending Made Easy*, Palmer-Pletsch Associates, 2008

Isark, M., *Supermarket Own Brand Guide: Choosing the Best Value Food and Drink*, Mitchell Beazley, 2006

Massingham Hart, R., *Dirt Cheap Gardening*, Storey Books, 1995

Mills, B. and Ross, A., *Cheap. Fast. Good!*, Workman Publishing, 2005

Morris, D.S., *Furniture Repair Tips That Save You Time and Money*, Phoenix Press Ltd, 2004

Murrin, O., *101 Money Saving Meals*, Hylas Publishing, 2003

Mustoe, J. and Mustoe I., *Penny Pincher's Book: Easy Ways of Living Better for Less*, Souvenir Press, 1995

Ott, S., Rawlings, E. and Warwick, R., *Grow Your Own Fruit and Veg in Plot, Pots or Growbags*, Foulsham, 2008

Prince, R., *The Savvy Shopper*, HarperPerennial, 2006

Reader's Digest, *New Complete Guide to Sewing: Step-by-Step Techniques for Making Clothes and Home Accessories*, Reader's Digest, 2003

Sanders, D. and Buller, D., *Part-Time Profits from Home*, Haynes Publications, 1997

Scheckel, P., *Home Energy Diet*, New Society Publishers, 2005

Scott, N., *Reduce, Reuse, Recycle!*, Green Books, 2004

Smith, A. and Baird, N., *Save Cash and Save the Planet*, Collins, 2005

Stouffer, T., *The 'Everything' Budgeting Book*, Adams Media Corporation, 2008

Sweet, M., *Infusions: Making Flavoured Oils, Vinegars and Spirits*, Chronicle Books, 1999

Williams, A.M., Jeppson, P.R. and Botkin, S.C., *Money Mastery: How to Control Spending, Eliminate Debt and Maximize Your Savings*, Career Press, 2002

Wilson, A., *The Consumer Guide to Home Energy Savings: Save Money, Save the Earth*, New Society Publishers, 2007

Websites

This is just a selection of some of the many useful websites discussed in the book.

Cashback
www.cashbackkings.com
www.greasypalm.co.uk
www.Quidco.com
www.Rpoints.com
www.topcashback.co.uk

Financial Advice
www.cashquestions.com
www.citizensadvice.org.uk
www.financialadvice.co.uk
www.moneyfacts.co.uk
www.moneysavingexpert.com
www.nationaldebtline.co.uk
www.unbiased.co.uk

Food and Drink
www.art-of-brewing.co.uk
www.eattheseasons.co.uk
www.homewinemaking.co.uk
www.lovefoodhatewaste.com
www.toptable.co.uk

Freebies
www.freebielist.com
www.free-stuff.co.uk
www.foodfreebies.co.uk
www.searchfreebies.co.uk

Holidays
www.bedandbreakfasts.co.uk
www.campingandcaravanningclub.co.uk
www.daysoutuk.com
www.homelink.org.uk
www.lastminute.com
www.laterooms.com
www.teletext.co.uk
www.yha.org.uk

Price Comparison
www.confused.com
www.gocompare.com
www.kelkoo.co.uk
www.moneysupermarket.com
www.mySupermarket.co.uk
www.pricerunner.co.uk
www.shopping.com
www.tescocompare.com
www.uswitch.com

Recycling and Swapping
www.bigwardrobe.com
www.freecycle.org
www.gumtree.com
www.readitswapit.co.uk
www.swapitshop.com
www.whatsmineisyours.com

Shopping
www.amazon.co.uk
www.asos.com
www.cdwow.com
www.costco.co.uk
www.ebay.co.uk
www.makro.co.uk
www.play.com

Travel
www.carshare.com
www.liftshare.org
www.megabus.com
www.nationalexpress.co.uk
www.nationalrail.co.uk
www.petrolprices.com
www.railcard.co.uk
www.tfl.gov.uk
www.whatcar.co.uk

Utilities
www.boilerjuice.co.uk
www.cheapest-utility-suppliers.co.uk
www.energysavingtrust.org.uk
www.fone-deals.co.uk
www.savewatersavemoney.co.uk
www.saynoto0870.com

Vouchers and Promotions
www.dealscentre.co.uk
www.hotukdeals.co.uk
www.myvouchercodes.co.uk
www.sendmediscounts.co.uk
www.shopcodes.co.uk
www.voucherheaven.com

Index

A

Air Travel Couriers 163
airports 199–200
all-inclusive deals 188
Ann Summers parties 236–37
Annual Percentage Rate (APR) 37–38
ant killers 135
anti-virus software 97
antibacterial cleaning 129
antiques 90–91, 227
Any Question Answered 235
armchairs 93
Association of Home Information
  Pack Providers (AHIPP) 35
attractions 184

B

B&Bs 185
  abroad 194
  providing 229
baby food 106
baby presents 241
babysitting services 237
baggage 190–91
bank accounts
  holiday money 191
  savings protection 55
  secure websites 86
  spring-cleaning 48
bank charges 50
bank loans 42–43
bankruptcy 61
beautician, becoming a 234
beer 219
  make you own 118, 220
benefits 50
birthdays
  birthday clubs 222
  card making 240
  celebrations 249–50
  parties 245–46
  presents 240–44, 247–49
  spending less 250–51
board games 217
BOGOF 109, 110
boiler cover 141–42
boot fairs 51
bottled water 115, 220
breakdown cover 172
broadband 146–49

budget shops 70–71, 119–22
budgets 48–52
bulk purchases 110
buses 153–54, 156, 198–99

C

cake making 243
camping 186
car boot sales 90–91
card making 240
cars
  buying 165–70
  car-sharing 177–78
  clubs 178–79
  finance 43, 170
  fuel economy 166, 174–75
  hire 179, 200
  insurance 45, 170–74
  tax 166–68, 177
  washing 179
cashback cards 79–80, 176
cashback sites 84–85
CDs 92, 246
celebrations 249–51
champagne 121
chargeback scheme 86
charity shops 90–91, 223
cheese 109
Child Trust Fund 60
children
  entertainment 216, 220–22,
    245–46
  food 106
  goods 94
  health 134
  presents 241
  swap shops 94
  travel 154, 157, 199
Christmas 67, 248, 251
cinemas 212, 222
Citizens Advice Bureau 58
classified ads 226
cleaning products 126–30
clothes
  cheap stores 70–71
  sales 248
  tips 222–23
  websites 85
coach travel 156, 198–99
coffee 102, 220

coke, cleaning with 129
comparison sites 107
competitions 236
compost heaps 135
computers 94–97, 146–49
Consumer Credit Act 37, 43, 86
Consumer Credit Counselling Service 58
contact lenses 77
cooking 100–101, 242
counterfeit goods 88
courier flights 163, 202
Credit Action 59
credit cards
  0 per cent purchase cards 40
  abroad 191
  cashback 39–40
  cutting down 38–39
  good practice 38–39
  as loyalty card 79
  online shopping 86
  pitfalls 37–38
  reward schemes 176
credit rating 22, 39
currency exchange 191
curtains 139
Cycle to Work scheme 152–53
cycling 206

D

debit cards 86
debt advice 27, 58–61
Debt Management Plans (DMPs) 61
decorating 131–33
Deed of Trust 31
delicatessens 103
dinner parties 246
direct debits 48, 136
discounts
  shopping 72–73
  travelling 155–57
dongles 148–49
dormant accounts 51
double glazing 139
draught-proofing 139
dress agencies 92
drinking 219–20
driveway parking 230
driving 175
DVD production 244
DVD rental 84, 216

E

eating out 214–15, 250
eBay 87–89, 226
electrical goods 47, 67, 68
    second-hand 91
electricity 136–42
energy 136–42
equity release 28–29
estate agents 32, 35
exchange rates 191
exercise 206–10
extended warranties 47
extensions 36
eyecare 76–77

F

fakes 88
family trees 244
fashion
    cheap stores 70–71
    sales 248
    tips 222–23
    websites 85
ferries 164
film locations 230
Financial Services Compensation
    scheme (FSCS) 55
firewalls 97
first-time buyers 30–33
fixed rate mortgages 25
flights 163–64, 201–3
flower arranging 232–33
flowers 242
food
    bulk buying 110–11
    cutting the cost 100–109
    for free 114–18
    planning 113
    supermarket tricks 112–14
football 209, 211–12
free food 114–18
free stuff 94–97, 152–57, 247–48
freezing food 109
frequent flyers 164
frozen food 104
fruit and veg 102–3, 108
    grow your own 114–15, 134–35
fuel economy 166, 174–75
furniture
    cheap stores 70
    haggling 72
    make do and mend 93
    second-hand 90–91
    websites 86

G

games 209–10
garages, renting out 230
gardening 134–35
gardens, selling 230
gas 136–42
gifts 243–44
glasses 76–77
golf 210
group travel 156–57

H

haggling 72–73
hairdressing 223
hanging baskets 135
health clubs 207
herbs 135
holidays
    abroad 187–203
    accommodation 184–85,
        193–94, 200
    camping 186
    credit cards 38
    at home 182–86
    transport 197–203
Home Information Packs (HIPs) 35
home working 231–36
homebuying tips 29–33
homelessness 59
homeselling tips 34–35
hostels 194
hotels
    abroad 193–94
    airports 200
    UK 184–85
house swaps 195–96

I

Independent Financial Advisers
    (IFAs) 23–24
Individual Voluntary Agreement (IVA) 61
insulation 138–39
insurance
    best deals 45–46
    boiler cover 141–42
    car insurance 45, 170–74
    necessity 44–45
    policies to avoid 46–47
    travel insurance 192
interest-only mortgage deals 26
investments 53, 56–57, 236
ironing 140
    for money 235
ISAs 53

K

Key Retirement Solutions 29
knitting 241

L

late bookings 188–89
lavatory paper 69
leisure 211–20
lemon juice 127
libraries 216–17, 220, 246
lift sharing 177
lights 140
limescale removal 129
loans 42–43
local papers 226–27
London 154
loyalty cards 78–79, 176, 248
luggage 190–91

M

make do and mend 93
markets 118
marrows 134
meat 103
medicines 74–76
mending 93
mobile phones 47, 146–49
money-off vouchers 71
mortgage brokers 23–24
Mortgage Payment Protection
    Insurance (MPPI) 46
mortgages
    brokers 23–24
    deposits 21–22
    fixed rate 25
    homebuying tips 29–33
    making money for 229–30
    repayment problems 25–29
Mother's Day 248
motoring 165–79
museums 183
music 92
music lessons 232

N

National Debtline 58
no-claims bonus 173
0 per cent purchase cards 80–81

O

oil suppliers 141
olive oil 121
online shopping 82–89, 104
operating systems 96
outlet shopping 71
overdrafts 50

P

packed lunches 101
painting 132–33
pan cleaners 129
parking 200
    driveway parking 230
parking penalties 177
parks 183
parties 246, 249–50
Pass Plus 174
passengers 177
passports 189–90
Payment Protection Insurance (PPI) 46
PayPal 87
personal care 74–77
personal finance 20
    advice and solutions 58–61
    budget 48–52
    credit cards 37–41
    home 21–29
    homebuying tips 29–33
    homeselling tips 34–36
    insurance 44–47
    investments 56–57
    loans 42–43
    savings 53–55
pet sitting 237
petrol 174–76, 200
phones 146–49
    abroad 192–93
photos 243–44
postage 249
potatoes 135
pre-paid credit cards 41
premium phone numbers 149
prescriptions 74–75
present buying 247–51
pumice 129

R

rail fares 158–62
railcards 155–57, 198
reading 216–17, 220
recipes 120
recycling 246
    presents for free 247–48
refurbished goods 92
rent out a room 27–28, 228
renting parking 200
renting property 33
repairs 93
restaurants 214–15, 250
reward schemes 176
runner beans 134
running 207

S

Sale and Rent Back schemes 28
sales 248
savings 21, 53–55
second-hand goods 90–92, 249
secure websites 86
secured loans 43
self-catering 185–86
sell-by dates 107
selling from home 226–29
sewing 93, 223, 242
    for money 233–44
shampoo 70
shared-ownership schemes 30–31
Shelter 59
SHIP (Safe Home Income Plan) 29
shopbots 82–83
shopping lists 113
shopping rules 64–67
showers 143–44
skin creams 69
sleeper trains 162
smoking 218–19
sofa sleeping 196
sofas 72, 90, 93
software 94–97
special offers 113
speeding tickets 172
sports 209–12
stain removers 129–30
standing orders 48
stock 108
stocks and shares 53, 56–57
    from home 236
storage 230
store cards 81
students 149, 154, 191, 193, 194, 196
supermarket shopping
    budget shops 68–70, 119–22
    bulk buying 110–11
    comparison sites 107
    damaged goods 107–8
    fruit and veg 102–3
    reward schemes 176
    timimg 107
    tricks of trade 112–14
    value brands 104–5
    vouchers 184
swap shops 92, 223
sweets 114
swimming 208

T

tax-free allowances 53
tax overpayments 50
tea tree oil 128

telesales 235
television 147–48, 215–16
tenants in common 31
theatres 212–13
theme parks 184
thermostats 138
third-party cover 173
trainers, cleaning 128
trains 158–62
    to airports 197–98
travel auctions 201–3
travel insurance 192
travelling
    to airports 197–200
    discounts 155–57
    for free 152–57
tutoring 232
TV audiences 215
TV shows 215
typing 234
tyre pressures 175
tyres 177

V

value brands 104–5
vegetarian dishes 102
Vehicle Excise Duty 166–68
vending machines 101–2
vinegar, cleaning with 128
voucher codes 247
vouchers
    money-off vouchers 71
    supermarkets 184
    voucher codes 84, 247

W

walking 152, 206
Warm Front scheme 141
washing services 234
water, bottled 115, 220
water softeners 128
water use 143–45
website design 231
wedding cakes, making 233
wedding gifts 244
wholesalers 111
window cleaner 128–29
wine 109, 219
    make you own 118
working holidays 194–95
wrapping paper 67, 246, 248
writing 234, 240